# GOLD STANDARD

THE **GOLDEN STATE WARRIORS'** DOMINANT RUN TO THE 2017 CHAMPIONSHIP

Nhat V. Meyer/Staff

This book is book is available in quantity at special discounts for your group or organization.
For further information, contact:

**Triumph Books LLC**
814 North Franklin Street
Chicago, Illinois 60610
Phone: (312) 337-0747
www.triumphbooks.com

Printed in U.S.A.
Hardcover ISBN: 978-1-62937-533-5
Paperback ISBN: 978-1-62937-363-8

**Bay Area News Group**
Sharon Ryan, Publisher and President, Bay Area News Group
Neil Chase, Executive Editor, Bay Area News Group
Bert Robinson, Managing Editor, Bay Area News Group
Bud Geracie, Executive Sports Editor, Bay Area News Group

**Content packaged by Mojo Media, Inc.**
Joe Funk: Editor
Jason Hinman: Creative Director

Front cover photo by Nhat V. Meyer/Staff. Back cover photo by Jose Carlos Fajardo/Staff.

Nhat V. Meyer/Staff

# CONTENTS

# INTRODUCTION

## By Anthony Slater

The Warriors capped the greatest three-year run, record-wise, in regular season history with the greatest postseason, record-wise, in NBA history: 16-1, a three-sweep stampede to the Finals and then a powerful 4-1 dismantling of LeBron James' Cavaliers. Folks will remember this 2017 playoff dominance.

But it began back in 2009. More specifically: June 25, 2009, draft day, when the Warriors almost unwisely traded their No. 7 overall pick for an aging Amare Stoudemire, but instead decided to keep it and select a skinny, small-college point guard who had the makings of a high-level shooter, but never a star. Right?

Everything about this Warriors rise starts with Steph Curry's stunning ascension to MVP level greatness. His arrival in the Bay Area is the starting point for this unlikely in-progress dynasty, the tiny shove of this snowball down the hill.

But the franchise was still in need of a facelift.

Joe Lacob's ownership group took over in November 2010, infusing money, resources and brainpower into an NBA market with untapped advantages. By sport's standards, it didn't take long to sprout.

Klay Thompson was selected in June of 2011, a smart pick at 11th overall that fit the league's trend toward 3-point shooting and defensive versatility. Thompson paired perfectly as the bigger guard in a backcourt that could spread the floor wider and defenses thinner than any in basketball history. The Splash Brothers were born.

Other pieces were still needed to reach the next level.

The biggest came in June 2012, the third time in four drafts that Warriors management snagged a future All-Star at an uncommon slot, this one coming far outside the lottery: Draymond Green, 35th overall. The backbone of a future title team was completed.

But the Finals MVP from their first championship hadn't arrived yet. The Warriors worked out an offseason sign-and-trade with the Denver Nuggets in the summer of 2013, shedding salary and losing future first-round picks, but obtaining Andre Iguodala, who, a year later, would willingly accept a Sixth Man role for which he was overqualified, rounding out the rotation.

The Warriors' rise from two decades in the ashes isn't only about the players. It's been about the culture — a top-down transparent, laid-back, egalitarian environment that has fostered a fun, free-spirited, pass-happy brand of basketball. That stems from Steve Kerr, hired in 2014 and paired with Bob Myers to form the head coach-general manager combo most likely to go on a surfing trip together.

Everyone noticed, including future free agents. Iguodala admitted the Warriors' style caught his eye the year before he joined them. A couple years before he hit the open market, Kevin Durant became intrigued with the team, the franchise, the Bay Area and the idea of playing for them all.

"When you play freely and have fun with the game, it just touches a lot of people," Durant said.

So there they all were in the Hamptons on July 1, 2016: Curry, Lacob, Thompson, Green, Iguodala, Kerr and Myers — the seven people most instrumental in this ascension. They were there to recruit Durant, the final piece to a team that has just made postseason history. Months earlier, they'd claimed a regular season record 73 wins, but a flameout in the Finals — they had a 3-1

Warriors' superstars Steph Curry and Kevin Durant embrace after fulfilling their goal of an NBA championship. (Jose Carlos Fajardo/Staff)

lead! — had provided enough motivation to add another superstar to their already loaded roster.

"When they came into the meeting, I was really looking for that energy and I felt it from the beginning," Durant said. "It was just so pure. It was a feeling I couldn't ignore. I wanted to be a part of it. No matter what happened, I wanted to be a part of it."

Curry was the megastar who started it all, yet was willing to share the superstar spotlight, sealing the deal with a welcoming text message. Thompson was the quiet assassin who, in a strange twist of fate, had made Durant's exit from Oklahoma City possible by slaying the Thunder a month earlier with 11 3s in the game of his life, changing the course of NBA history.

Green was the lead recruiter, Durant's closest friend on the team, persistent in his luring, convincing Durant that this was the right place for him as both a player and human. Lacob was the money man. Kerr and Myers were the architects who connected with Durant on a personal level, preaching the joy of basketball but also the importance of life beyond the game.

Iguodala was the example that most fit Durant, the only one of the assembled players who wasn't drafted by the Warriors, a wiser veteran that had experienced life in different organizations and NBA cities, had sacrificed glory by coming off the bench and could best give a wider-lens assessment. His conversation with Durant might have been one of the most important.

"It's just like going to college," Iguodala said. "How do I see myself on campus? How do I see myself with other students? What's my major on the side? It's a similar process as going to college. This is a place where you combine all media and basketball interests as far as Silicon Valley and tech."

Durant pulled the trigger, bolted for the Bay, absorbed the backlash and formed a megateam of stars — four of them in their direct prime — that all melded ideally into this era of 3s, defensive versatility and playmaking from every position.

The result: a 16-1 stampede to the title, the best playoff record in NBA history, and a second title in three years. ∎

Kevin Durant's dominant series earned him his first NBA title, as well as his first Finals MVP trophy. (Nhat V. Meyer/Staff)

JUNE 1, 2017 • OAKLAND, CALIFORNIA
WARRIORS 113, CAVALIERS 91

# STAR POWER

## Warriors Ride Durant, Curry and a Huge Turnover Advantage to Lopsided Win

### By Anthony Slater

Klay Thompson's shooting woes worsened, Draymond Green didn't score until late in the third quarter, and Zaza Pachulia led a brigade of first-half missed layups. But the Warriors, while not perfect, were still dominant in Game 1 of the NBA Finals, blasting the Cleveland Cavaliers 113-91 at Oracle Arena.

How? They transformed their two typical flaws into major advantages and rode their two MVPs — one dunking on the world, the other bombing away deep 3s — to a 13th straight playoff win, the 11th by double-digits, upping their average postseason margin of victory to 16.7 per game.

"They're the best I've ever seen," Cavs coach Tyronn Lue said. "I mean, no other team has done this, right? 13-0."

To beat the Warriors this season, and it's been done only 15 times in 95 games, you need to turn them over and beat them up on the glass. The Cavaliers did that on Christmas, grabbing 18 offensive rebounds and forcing 19 turnovers, which helped them edge the Warriors by one.

But in Game 1, the Warriors had more second-chance points (18 to 13) and won the turnover battle by an astounding 20-4 margin. Those four turnovers were the fewest the Warriors have committed all season. Their previous low was seven.

"When you turn the ball over against this team, they become impossible to guard," Draymond Green said. "It's LeBron (James) coming downhill, Kyrie (Irving) coming downhill with a bunch of shooters around them. So we knew coming into this game, we had to value the basketball."

That monster advantage gave the Warriors 20 more shot attempts than the Cavaliers (106 to 86). And when you give the Warriors' historically efficient offense that many more chances, even when all parts are not operating optimally, the mountain is too steep to climb.

Especially when Kevin Durant and Stephen Curry are standing at the top drop-kicking you off.

"You cannot simulate what they bring to the table," James said. "No matter how many days you have off, you can't simulate that."

Durant served as the night's star in his loud return to the NBA Finals. The Cavaliers' defense, bottom 10 in the league this season and not that much better in the playoffs, helped get him going. Twice in the first half, with Curry flanking and spreading out to the wing on a fast break, Durant galloped up the floor with those long limbs, looked toward Curry and both Irving and J.R. Smith fled the lane as Durant soared for unharmed dunks.

Steph Curry drives to the basket with Cleveland's Tristan Thompson guarding him in Game 1. Curry had 28 points, six rebounds and 10 assists in the comfortable win. (Dan Honda/Staff)

"Our game plan was backwards," Lue said. "When Kevin Durant has the ball, you don't want to leave him."

But Durant dunked plenty of times against slightly more imposing defensive efforts. Durant shook LeBron to the ground on a quick-twitch pump and go move for a slam, powered through Irving for a layup — his first eight makes were all at the rim — and then forced his way to the free throw line a few times late in the first half, putting up 23 in the first 24 minutes.

The Warriors outscored the Cavaliers 56-30 in the paint. Durant finished with a game-high 38 — finally busting out his 3-point shot late to cap his huge night.

But Curry never had to get hot from 3 because he just stayed hot, carrying over his scorching stroke from the last round to plant six of his 11 threes in Game 1, giving him an NBA-high 59 made 3s in 13 playoff games. The Cavaliers' Kevin Love is the next closest shooter, with 41 makes in 14 games.

Curry finished with 28 points and 10 assists — he didn't have more than six assists during any Finals game last year — giving him 66 combined points with Durant, as the two catapulted some of their struggling teammates to the rout.

Pachulia either passed up or butchered three first-half layups, before making a pair of circus shots in the second half.

Thompson played terrific defense but shot three of 16 and missed all five of his 3s as his massive shooting slump worsened.

Green only made three of his 12 shots.

But the Warriors are up 1-0, in dominant fashion, because they protected the ball, won the battle on the glass and let their two stars shine.

"We could be a lot better than we were tonight," Durant said. "But in The Finals, you take the W." ■

Cleveland's Kyrie Irving tries to split the double team in the fourth quarter of the Cavs' Game 1 loss. Irving had 24 points on 22 shots in the sizeable Warriors win. (Jose Carlos Fajardo/Staff)

JUNE 4, 2017 • OAKLAND, CALIFORNIA
WARRIORS 132, CAVALIERS 113

# BIG 'D' IN DURANT

## He Scores 33 and Blocks Cavs' Path in Blowout

### By Anthony Slater

LeBron James had powerfully dragged the Cavaliers into a competitive fight in Game 2, but for a chance at an upset, he needed a sliver of help in the final eight minutes to take this series back to Cleveland tied.

So the Cavaliers cleared out and posted up Kevin Love on the thinner Kevin Durant. Love nailed Durant with a few power dribbles and rugged shoulders to the chest, but couldn't move him much. So the big man settled for a 10-foot hook shot, a low-percentage look if he even got it off.

But he didn't get it off. Durant rose with those tarantula arms and completely ate Love's hook shot, palming it, staring Love down and then starting a fastbreak the other way. It was Durant's fifth, final and most emphatic block, serving as the punctuation point of the Warriors' 132-113 Game 2 win, sending them to Cleveland with a commanding 2-0 series lead.

"Kev's defense was unreal," Steve Kerr said. "Probably the key to the whole game."

This latest Warrior win — pushing them to a record 14-0 in the playoffs — had everything:

• A Steve Kerr return to the sidelines, announced a couple hours before tip.

• A Stephen Curry triple-double, highlighted by a masterful dribbling exhibition that spun LeBron James into a circle before he scooped in a layup over his sledgehammer block attempt.

• A Klay Thompson breakout, his first game with four 3s since the first round against the Blazers, finishing the night with 22 points on only 12 shots.

But on a night where Draymond Green's foul trouble sapped his usual impact and saddled him on the bench, Durant's two-way dominance may have been the game's most important factor.

To start the second and fourth quarters, when Green typically anchors the Warriors' second-unit, Steve Kerr found his versatile forward in foul trouble. But he wanted to remain with a smaller lineup, pushing the pace and forcing Cleveland into matchup issues.

So he turned to Durant, riding him for a playoff-high 41 minutes and uncorking him as the center, something the Warriors have done very little of this season. It's something they never could've done with Harrison Barnes, who is the size of a normal small forward. But Durant is a 7-foot pterodactyl, who has only gained strength and defensive guile during his first decade in the league.

Kevin Durant stuffs home two of his 33 points in Game 2. In a tremendous all-around performance, Durant also added 13 rebounds, six assists, three steals and five blocks. (Ray Chavez/Staff)

"I don't think there are many teams in the league where their backup (small-ball center) is better than their starter," Green said. "So I think that's a luxury we have with KD ... To say pick up the slack is kind of a ridiculous term because he's a great player, an MVP, one of the best players in the world. So with me going out, it wasn't like we were going to skip a beat with him right there taking over my minutes."

Durant delivered his first highlight sequence midway through the first quarter. After Kyrie Irving slithered past Klay Thompson and sprung temporarily free for a 12-footer, Durant swooped in from the help-side to swat away the jumper. He scooped up the loose ball, pushed it upcourt and planted a transition 3. Then he backpedalled on defense and, moments later, ripped away LeBron's dribble for one of his three steals.

"When Draymond went out, I just tried to do my best to help everybody out," Durant said. "He's so good at just sniffing out plays before they happen. And so I just tried to follow his lead with that. I learned so much from him throughout the season."

That was only the first of Durant's five blocks. He stoned a Channing Frye pick-and-roll layup attempt later in the first quarter, swiped a LeBron James' driving floater out of bounds in the second quarter and rose to redirect an Iman Shumpert flying dunk attempt in the third, just after Green had left the game and he pushed to the center spot.

But nothing was quite as emphatic or symbolic of his defensive dominance than that fourth quarter block on Love. After a Cavaliers run, the Warriors had redirected momentum, pushed up 16 and were in need of one more big play to put LeBron and the lingering Cavaliers away.

Love went to the power dribble and soft hook. Then Durant rose, completely erased it and scooped up the loose ball.

"They think they got a mismatch and they're trying to go at K in the post and he blocked the shot, get the rebound," Draymond Green smiled.

Then Durant stopped for a moment and, in celebration, yelled in Love's direction.

"See, that's the big part for me, you know, he blocks a shot and start talking," Green said. "That's what got me hyped."

But Durant wasn't done. After enjoying the block for a second or two, he dribbled into the frontcourt, whizzed right by LeBron James with a crossover and then floated in a

Klay Thompson draws the foul on Kevin Love in the first quarter of the Game 2 blowout. Thompson contributed an efficient 22 points on eight of 12 shooting from the floor. (Ray Chavez/Staff)

bank shot over a helpless Love. It put the Warriors up 18. It essentially put the game to rest.

Durant carried over his offensive rhythm from Game 1, scoring 33 points, sending down a couple emphatic dunks, nailing four 3s and handing out six assists. He made six of his nine shots when guarded by LeBron James, who otherwise imposed his will on this game.

"He took some contact and still finished the play," Green said. "Those are the plays that kind of put you over the top, the plays that just bring life into a team. That's the luxury that you have with K, where he get a block, he get the rebound, he don't have to give the ball to nobody, he can go get a bucket. That was a huge play for us. Like you said, I think that's where we kind of closed the game out with that play right there."

In all, Durant finished with 33 points, 13 rebounds, six assists and those five blocks, joining Tim Duncan and Ralph Sampson as the only players to put up those stats in a playoff game. Add his three steals and Durant delivered a stat-line never seen in NBA history. ■

Above: Kevin Durant is congratulated by teammates as he comes to the bench in the fourth quarter of the win. (Ray Chavez/Staff)
Opposite: Kevin Durant snares a rebound surrounded by Cavs, one of his 13 boards in the game. (Ray Chavez/Staff)

**NBA FINALS • GAME 3**

JUNE 7, 2017 • CLEVELAND, OHIO

WARRIORS 118, CAVALIERS 113

# SHOT AT HISTORY

## Stunning Comeback Places Warriors One Win from Title

### By Anthony Slater

The Warriors survived the Cavaliers' powerful Game 3 counterpunch and, in doing so, are now just an inch away from the most sparkling run to an NBA title in history.

Trailing for much of the second half, the Warriors clawed back in the fourth quarter and beat the Cavaliers 118-113, bumping them up 3-0 in these NBA Finals, pushing them to 15-0 in these playoffs and planting them on the doorstep of unprecedented playoff perfection.

Of the 15 wins, this was the toughest. LeBron James was a human freight train the entire night, going off for 39 points and coming one assist shy of a triple-double. And unlike the first two games, he finally had help from his co-star, Kyrie Irving, who scored 38 on a number of slithery moves and creative finishes at the rim.

But in the end, it was the Warriors' stars who survived a raucous environment, a two-pronged offensive attack and a seven-point fourth quarter hole, erasing many of the demons that plagued them from a season ago.

"I played against some great teams, but I don't think any team has had this type of firepower," James said. "So even when you're playing well, you got to play like A-plus plus."

Steph Curry was incredible much of the night, going for 26 points, a team-high 13 rebounds, six assists and only one turnover. Klay Thompson parlayed his huge Game 2 into a bigger Game 3, nailing six of the Warriors' 16 3-pointers and hitting 30 points for the first time in this postseason. He kept them afloat early.

But Kevin Durant, the front-runner for Finals MVP, drove the Warriors home in the final sequence.

With less than two minutes left, the Warriors trailed by four and their perfect playoffs were in peril. But with 1:15 left, Durant powerfully pushed Kevin Love back on a drive, got to about 12 feet out and planted a floater to pull the Warriors within two.

On the ensuing possession, Kyle Korver got a decent look at a 3 from the corner, which would've put the Cavaliers back up five with less than a minute left.

But the sharpshooter bricked the shot that will likely haunt his offseason memories. Durant climbed high for the defensive rebound and then, six seconds later, made maybe the biggest shot of his storied career.

Durant pushed the rebound into the frontcourt and, without hesitation, bounced into a deep transition 3 over LeBron James. LeBron rose to try to bother the shot but did so cautiously.

"The last thing I want to do is foul a jump shooter," James said. "So I wanted to jump and contest it, but I

Kevin Durant goes up for the basket while LeBron James looks on. Durant had another huge game, with 31 points, eight rebounds and four assists. (Jose Carlos Fajardo/Staff)

know he shoots, he kind of leans forward a little bit. So I just stayed there, high hands, contested."

Didn't matter. Durant drilled it, the most important shot of his career, putting the Warriors up 114-113 with 45 seconds left.

"He took over," coach Steve Kerr said. "You can tell, he knows this is his moment. He's been an amazing player in this league for a long time, and I think he's — he senses this is his time, his moment."

On the next possession, trailing by one, Irving tried to go to work on Klay Thompson, who has dogged him the entire series.

After a failed drive attempt, Irving eventually found himself backing up to that same spot on the right wing where he won the NBA Finals last year.

But despite Irving's offensive exploits on this night — he was 16 of 22 on two-point shots — he was 0 of 7 from three. That seventh miss came with 26 seconds left when he left the pull-back 3 short.

"I'll be replaying that one for a while," Irving said.

Curry grabbed the huge rebound, his 13th, and Durant eventually received the ball and absorbed the foul. He hit both free throws, giving him seven points in 63 seconds — a personal 7-0 run that essentially won this game. The Warriors led by three.

But they still needed one more stop. After a timeout, the Cavaliers drew up a play to get James a corner 3. James navigated into that spot, caught, turned and set up to fire.

But Andre Iguodala, who has had a quiet postseason, made the biggest defensive play of the night, stripping LeBron and knocking it off his leg out of bounds. Curry got the ensuing inbounds, absorbed the automatic foul and made the game-sealing free throws.

"We just kept our poise (in the fourth quarter)," Iguodala said. "In the past, we kind of got haywire and hectic."

Perfection is one game away.

"It's not over," Durant said. "The job's not done. Closeout games are the toughest." ∎

JaVale McGee blocks a shot by Cleveland Cavaliers' big man Tristan Thompson. Thompson continued his poor play in the series and was a non-factor in Game 3, with zero points and three rebounds in 23 minutes. (Jose Carlos Fajardo/Staff)

**NBA FINALS • GAME 4**

JUNE 9, 2017 • CLEVELAND, OHIO

CAVALIERS 137, WARRIORS 116

# NO SWEEP 16

## Record-Setting Cavs Ruin Warriors' Quest for Perfect Postseason

### By Anthony Slater

The Warriors' chance at playoff perfection died right before the finish line. Now their shot at redemption will have to wait at least a few more days.

In one of the wildest NBA games in recent memories, the Cavaliers pounced on the Warriors early, shot themselves to a huge lead and staved off a sweep during an emotional — and often unhinged — second half, finishing off the Warriors 137-116 to move this series to 3-1 heading back to Oakland.

In their three previous Game 4s during these playoffs, all sweep-completers, the Warriors buried dejected Western Conference opponents, leading the Blazers by 23, the Jazz by 22 and the Spurs by 12 after the first quarter.

It was the opposite on Friday night. The Cavaliers erupted right from the tip, scoring 14 points in the first two-and-a-half minutes, spiking out to their first double-digit lead of the series in a flash.

"We were not sharp defensively and they got it rolling," Warriors coach Steve Kerr said. "They brought a level of physicality that we did not match."

Then the Warrior fouls started to pile up. They had 10 in the first six minutes. Klay Thompson, Andre Iguodala and Stephen Curry each had two fouls in the first 10 minutes.

The Cavaliers shot 22 free throws in the first quarter, which served as the backbone of the best offensive quarter in Finals history, done against the NBA's best defense during these playoffs.

"You got to give them credit," Draymond Green said. "They were aggressive, but when everyone has two fouls, it's hard to match the physicality."

The Cavaliers made 14 free throws, hit seven of their 12 first-quarter 3s, made 14 of their 24 shots and scored a record 49 first-quarter points, jumping out to a 16-point lead on a shellshocked Warriors team, absorbing and staggering from the biggest punch they've faced in these playoffs.

"We gave up a game's worth of points in the first half," David West said.

Things somewhat stabilized in the second quarter, as the Cleveland lead fluctuated between 10 and 20. The Warriors scored 35 points in the quarter, but their defense remained a problem, ceding another 37 to the Cavaliers, who put up a record 86 in the first half. The Cavs led by 18 at the break and finished the night with a Finals record 24 made 3s.

"I don't envision them coming to Oracle and hitting 24 3s," Green said.

Some of it was because of breakdowns, but plenty of

Shaun Livingston (34) and Stephen Curry react to a technical foul called against Draymond Green during a contentious Game 4. (Nhat V. Meyer/Staff)

it was ridiculous shot-making by a desperate Cavaliers team, determined to not let the Warriors celebrate on their home floor for a second time in three years.

They hit 13 3s in the first half — more than they had in any of the first three games — and LeBron James got his most help of the series, including six 3s from Kevin Love, solid minutes from Richard Jefferson and a second straight monster offensive night from Kyrie Irving, who scored 40.

The streaky Cavaliers' point guard made 15 of his 27 shots, often slithering by and shedding sturdy Thompson defense to drop crazy shots from tough angles. In Games 3 and 4, Irving made an astounding 31 shots on 56 attempts after making only 18 of 45 during the first two games in Oakland.

Much like the second quarter, the Cavaliers' lead fluctuated between 10 and 20 throughout the second half. But the lack of a close game didn't strip the night of its drama in the last 24 minutes. That included some scuffles and controversies that nearly escalated to ugly levels.

Included: Kevin Durant and James yelling at each other (and picking up technicals) during a review of a flagrant foul delivered by Love on Durant.

Then later: a physical scrum for a loose ball detonated into a showdown between Zaza Pachulia and Iman Shumpert. As Shumpert stood over a fallen Pachulia and the two tussled after the whistle, Pachulia seemed to reach up and slap Shumpert near the groin area, inciting an argument.

During the aftermath and review, Pachulia got into a heated argument with a loud courtside fan right near the Warriors bench. Matt Barnes, Curry, Durant and West also had words, as security and police raced over to intervene and ensure it didn't escalate. The courtside fan was tossed.

"He was jaw-jacking with Zaza and it was fake, man," West said. "That little (expletive) ain't going to do nothing in real life."

Also in the second half: a mysterious ejection and then non-ejection of Green. In the first half, both Green and Kerr were disputing a foul call in the same area. One of the officials whistled for a technical. The scorer gave it to Green, but the referee apparently whistled it on Kerr.

Then in that third quarter, while arguing another foul, Green was hit with a second technical, which is an automatic ejection.

But then after some extended confusion, the crowd erupted in boos when they realized Green was still allowed to remain on the court. The eventual explanation: The first technical should have been given to Kerr, not Green, a strange reversal that served as the officiating lowlight during a controversial night.

But if there's one silver lining for the Warriors in a nightmare Game 4, it's that they exited the hostile and often emotional environment without an incident that could lead to a suspension of one of their main guns, like what happened to Green a season ago, completely altering the Finals.

"Thank God I get to play on Monday," Green said. "Hopefully."

Now the series shifts back to Oakland, where all the 3-1 ghosts and jokes await the Warriors as they try to finish this playoff run at redemption.

"I've won (a title) on the road," Green said. "I want to see how it feels to win one at home." ■

LeBron James and the Cavaliers were unstoppable in Game 4, putting up a record 49 points in the first quarter alone. (Jose Carlos Fajardo/Staff)

JUNE 12, 2017 • OAKLAND, CALIFORNIA
WARRIORS 129, CAVALIERS 120

# SWEET REVENGE

## Curry, Warriors Find Redemption in 2017 Championship

### By Marcus Thompson II

Stephen Curry, with his youngest daughter Ryan in his arms, ran onto the championship podium. Screaming into the sea of yellow, bouncing with joy.

This is what validation looks like.

"It's kinda hard to argue what I've done and what's going on here," Curry said, flashing a smile, acknowledging a rare moment of self-proclamation. "I will say that."

For nearly a calendar year, he has had to swallow the slights, the questions about his eliteness. He's been called overrated, classless, weak, soft, not-clutch, unworthy. And he just had to eat it.

It's the price of admission into the club of super-stardom. You must be doubted. You must be prodded. You must digest the hate and be better because of it. That's what the great ones do. You answer on the court.

And in the clincher, Curry had 34 points, 10 assists, six rebounds and enough moments to silence his loudest critics. The reasonable ones, anyway. He led the way to a 129-120 win over the Cavaliers, clinching the Warriors' second title in three years, completing their vengeance from last year's epic collapse.

"Steph is — I never seen nobody like him," Durant said. "I told him last night. I said, 'When you play with force, I never seen a player like you before.' And he played with force (in Game 5)."

This is how you earn top-tier status. Curry wasn't the Finals MVP. But he vindicated himself by averaging 26.8 points, 9.4 assists and 8.0 rebounds in an NBA Finals.

Curry's fingerprints were all over this game. He overcame early turnovers and struggles with his shooting. He controlled the game, as Steve Kerr kept the ball in his hands.

Perhaps most important, he set the table for Durant to shine. He uses his aggressiveness and three-point prowess to clear the way for Durant, as the two shared in more pick-and-rolls than we've seen from them.

It was a microcosm for the rare sacrifice he made, inviting Durant to the Warriors. Outside of the Bay Area, Durant is almost unanimously deemed the Warriors' best player.

But Curry built this whole thing. From the time the franchise was placed in his hands, he's carried these Warriors. And even with an amazing player next to him like Durant, it was still clear Curry is the engine of the Warriors.

His greatness looks different, especially next to Durant's jaw-dropping game. But Curry's game and

Stephen Curry and Kevin Durant share in the elation of achieving the Warriors' second NBA championship in three years, the first of Durant's career. (Nhat V. Meyer/Staff)

leadership are even more integral to the Warriors' success.

"The stuff you hear about Steph as far as sacrificing and being selfless and caring about his teammates, caring about other people is real," Durant said. "It's not a fake. It's not a facade. He doesn't put on this mask or this suit every single day to come in here and fake in front of you guys. He really is like that. And it's amazing to see a superstar who sacrifices, who doesn't care about nothing but the group."

But even that nuance wasn't enough. Curry needed to do what superstars do. And he did that this series, and in this closeout game.

And he sealed the performance in a fashion fit for a title run marked by revenge — alone, on the left wing, against Kyrie Irving.

Curry danced through a series of crossovers, avoiding Irving's swipes, as Oracle Arena lathered up in a frenzy. Curry then stepped back and rose up over Irving — the very player who set Curry off on this journey of reclaiming his status — and drilled the dagger 3-pointer. And Curry's answer was complete, his retort punctuated.

Moments later, even though there was still time on the clock, Curry couldn't contain his glee. He was jumping and screaming when he should have been bringing the ball up. This feeling was a long time coming for him.

It wasn't enough to just play well. Curry has done that in these Finals. It's playing well when all the marbles are on the line. When the world is waiting for you to produce, expecting magic from you.

People want to see his no-look pass to Andre Iguodala during a critical fourth-quarter stretch. They want to see three straight driving layups with the game on the line, answering the desperation of the best player in the game.

They want to see him come up with a timely interception in the fourth quarter during the game-ending run.

They want to see him have a counter when the Cavaliers take away his 3-pointer and his stroke isn't feeling the greatest. Instead of chucking away from deep like he did last year, Curry lived in the middle of the Cavaliers' defense. He was 8-for-11 inside the arc with 12 free throws.

On the biggest stage, and healthy, Curry proved he wasn't a flash in the pan. That his two MVPs and 2015 championship wasn't a fluke. Despite not having the freakish size of the likes of LeBron James and Kevin Durant, he proved he belongs. LeBron made it clear there is nobody in the NBA better than he. But there should be no more doubt Curry is in the mix with the game's elite.

Perhaps it was just a matter of time before he got here. Or maybe he needed to go through that collapse, feel the sting of not showing up, hear the jabs at his worth from across the nation, to become even better. Either way, the end result from this three-year run — two MVPs, 207 regular season wins, and two championships — is that he's here now.

This is what validation looks like. ∎

The Golden State Warriors, including co-owner Peter Guber and forward Draymond Green, hold up the NBA Finals trophy after the Warriors' 129-120 victory in Game 5. (Nhat V. Meyer/Staff)

# KEVIN DURANT CLAIMS FINALS MVP

## By Anthony Slater

Game 4 had erased the Warriors' chance at playoff perfection. Game 5 was attached to rising angst about a repeat of last June's collapse in the Finals.

But what always felt inevitable was finally made official late Monday night: the Warriors are NBA champions again, for the second time in three years, clinching the 2017 title with a 129-120 putaway of LeBron James and his powerful Cavaliers.

Before the final buzzer sounded, the Warriors shoveled the ball over to Kevin Durant, allowing him to dribble out the clock and bask in the moment, beginning an emotional celebration of the first major sports title won by a Bay Area team at home since 1974.

For Durant, this was the long-awaited NBA title No. 1, finally obtained in Year 10, playing for his second franchise. And in these Finals, it was well-earned. He had the dunk-fest in Game 1, the block-fest in Game 2, the iconic 3 in Game 3 and the loud closing statement to help seal Game 5, taking home the Finals MVP trophy.

"We did it," Durant shouted to his mother, Wanda, during a TV interview. "I told you when I was eight years old we'd do it!"

Later, he acknowledged the pressure of it all.

"I couldn't sleep for the last two days," he said. "I was anxious. I was jittery… We were really good tonight. But I've gotta tip my hat to Cleveland. LeBron and Kyrie, I've never seen two like them before."

The same could be said for Durant and Stephen Curry. Durant scored 39 points — he broke 30 in all five games of the Finals — and Curry had 34 and 10 assists.

And still, the Warriors led by only three points after LeBron James scored on the first possession of the fourth quarter. You could feel the nervousness circling the building.

But on the following possession, the Warriors just dumped it to Durant high up on the right post and he jab-stepped a defending LeBron and then planted a jumper right over him. The next time down, after a defensive stop, the Warriors went right back to the well and the Cavaliers, fearing the same result, tossed an extra help defender Durant's way.

Durant perfectly read the situation, fired a cross-court pass into Andre Iguodala's shooting pocket and the super-sub continued his huge night by burying a 3, jumping the lead back to eight.

The sequence summed up the series, a third version of Warriors-Cavaliers but the first with a Durant injection. Cleveland had an answer for plenty, but not Durant, not in the series-deciding moments.

Durant outplayed LeBron in Game 1, finishing with 38 points and zero turnovers. He backed it up with a 33-point, 13-rebound, 5-block Hakeem Olajuwon-like Game 2, stuffing a Kevin Love post-up to punctuate the dominant win.

Then in Game 3, with the series teetering between a competition and a steamroll, he ripped out Cleveland's hearts with a 7-0 run in the final minute, highlighted by the shot of his life — and he's made nearly 7,000 of them in the NBA — a 26-footer from the left wing, one of his favorite spots on the floor, released high above LeBron James' helpless contest.

Both Durant and the Warriors blew their first closeout chance in Game 4. But they were delivered a prime chance to vanquish that loss — and the 3-1 ghosts

Kevin Durant was tremendous throughout the series, scoring at least 30 points in each of the five games, while averaging 35.2 points, 8.4 rebounds, 5.4 assists and 1.6 blocks. (Ray Chavez/Staff)

that haunted them — at home in Game 5. And though the Cavaliers crawled and LeBron played unbelievably, they were helpless to Durant's lethal efficiency in the game's biggest moments, impossible to contain him amid the other stars the Warriors already had.

"I've got the best job in the world," said a teary-eyed coach Steve Kerr. "These guys are so gifted and so committed and so unselfish."

Kerr, who missed 11 of the 17 playoff games because of pain related to his 2015 back surgery, also saluted Mike Brown and the rest of his coaching staff for "keeping the ship sailing smoothly."

The Cavaliers had a strong start. But two Durant 3s helped bring the Warriors back in the first half. Then, as Cleveland tried to climb back in the second half, Durant continually delivered jab after jab to stagger the Cavaliers back.

Right after the pass to Iguodala to put the Warriors up eight, Durant nailed a 3 to erase the Kevin Love and-1 seconds prior. When a Kyle Korver 3 with 8:27

left cut it to six, Durant sliced backdoor for an easy dunk, uncontested just like the six dunks he had in the first half of Game 1.

In all, he made 14 of 20 shots, including five of eight from beyond the arc. For the series, he shot 56 percent from the field. He led the Warriors in rebounds and blocks.

And he dribbled out the clock in that final moment, sealing the win and then — after a congratulatory hug from LeBron — celebrated with his teammates and family. He got a hug from Stephen Curry. He got his TV interview interrupted by his mother: "Don't matter what nobody say, you did it," she told him.

Then he climbed on the stage and accepted the Finals MVP award, named after Bill Russell and delivered by Bill Russell, completing a first season with the Warriors that couldn't have played out any better.

"Great group of guys," Durant said. "Great community, great organization, great group of fans."

"Kevin," owner Joe Lacob said, "thanks for coming." ∎

# The Road To The Title

# PRESS COVERAGE INTENSE ON CURRY, DURANT & CO.

## More Than 200 Reporters From Across the Globe Flock to Biggest Media Day in Warriors History

### By Daniel Brown • September 27, 2016

There was no actual basketball played at Warriors media day. The only shots taken came from the clicking cameras documenting Kevin Durant's every long-legged step.

And so it began. The great NBA chemistry experiment is underway. Having fallen one game short of back-to-back titles, the Warriors responded by signing Durant, the biggest star on the market, and unleashing this: the biggest media day in Bay Area memory.

"I wouldn't say it's strange. It's new and fresh," Durant said. "I'm looking forward to it. I just got super excited as I was walking in here."

Durant wasn't the only one revved up. The Warriors issued a record number of press credentials this year, cutting things off at about 225 because there was no room left on the floor.

The usual alphabet soup of sports outlets were here — ESPN, TNT, NBA TV — but also CNBC, covering things from a technology angle. Several international outlets were on hand, meaning that Draymond Green quotes were being translated back to China, Turkey, France, Japan and Italy.

On one hand, there were a wide-array of questions ranging from the meaning of a Rick James tattoo (that one was for Durant) to attendance at yoga classes (Zaza Pachulia) to plans for the national anthem (every player).

But at the heart of it there was just one question: How will the Warriors bounce back from their epic collapse against the Cleveland Cavaliers in the NBA Finals?

"I don't want to walk in the door thinking about Game 7," Curry said, referring to the defeat last June 19 that capped the Cavs' comeback from down 3-1.

"Nobody should be thinking that way. But you should remember how you felt when you were walking off the floor. You should remember all that you did all summer to get yourself in a better position individually and collectively."

This year's Warriors will feature a quartet of All-Stars: Curry, Durant, Green and Klay Thompson.

They are basketball's Beatles — the Fab Four-iors — complete with the hype. But they insisted that they are ready for hoopla.

"We're used to the pressure," reserve guard Shaun Livingston said. "The stakes will be a lot higher this year than they were last year, just because of adding Kevin and the team that we have in place. But I've been on nine teams, and I know that there are worse situations to be in. I'm happy to have all these expectations. You'd rather have it this way than the other way."

Indeed, the chaotic scene prompted Raymond

Steph Curry speaks to a reporter during the Warriors' September 27, 2016 practice. (Anda Chu/Staff)

Ridder, the team's longtime vice president of communications, to reflect the bad ol' days. Once upon a time, the Warriors were such a non-story that Ridder and his communications staff would meet before the season and ask themselves: "What can we do to entice people to get interested in our basketball team?"

So they came up with gimmicks. One year, reporters could meet at Monta Ellis' house and hitch a ride to the press conference.

Any bright ideas this year?

"This year, the idea was: 'I'm sorry, you can't come,'" Ridder cracked.

Far from the days of hitching a ride with a player, Tim Bontemps of the *Washington Post* drove himself across the country. He piled into his 2009 Dodge Avenger last week and began high-tailing it across the country, 11 hours at a time.

For Bontemps, it was a one-way trip. He is one of several national reporters moving to the Bay Area for the season to embed with Golden State. *The New York Times*, Bleacher Report, *USA Today* and ESPN are also planning to cover the Warriors on a frequent basis.

"I really think the Warriors are going to be the dominant story line in sports over the next nine months," Bontemps said. "When you look at the American sporting landscape between now and June, it's hard for me to see a bigger story than what's going on with the Warriors on a daily basis."

But this year's Warriors tale has already taken a darker twist. They are no longer the cuddly Globetrotter clones featuring a Baby-Faced Assassin.

Critics now cast them as overrated chokers who became the first team in NBA history to blow a 3-to-1 lead in the Finals. The Warriors also lost their tempers along the way, with Curry chucking his mouth guard into the stands and Green emerging as a threat to groins everywhere.

Signing Durant to a two-year, $54.275 million deal in the offseason had the dual effect of creating a super-team and robbing Oklahoma City of the most beloved star it has ever known.

"Listen, the Warriors are going to be the most hated

Kevin Durant speaks with reporters during a preseason practice. The Warriors issued a record number of press credentials for the 2016-17 season. (Anda Chu/Staff)

team in the NBA this year. They're also going to be the most popular team," Bontemps said. "Every arena they go to, they're going to get booed unmercifully. And everyone across the country who is a neutral fan is going to be rooting against them.

"It's just the way our society works, right? It's just a lot more fun to see a Goliath get taken down."

Sam Amick, who covers the NBA for *USA Today,* has already felt reader backlash. He recently scored an extensive one-on-one interview with Curry, and parlayed that sit-down into several stories.

"And every single time I tweeted something about the story, there was some non-Warriors fan chiming in to say 'Whatever, they blew a 3-1 lead' — or even something more vulgar," Amick said. "Today I blocked a guy because he had something X-rated to say about Steph. … Certain fans resent the hype and the way (the Warriors) were talked about as an invincible team."

In the least, the Warriors seemed prepared for the media day onslaught, which was no small feat considering it's turned into a three-hour gamut. The itinerary included required stops at the Warriors social media hub, where players goofed around on Instagram, Facebook, Twitter and Snapchat and other apps born long after Bob Cousy.

Next up? The actual basketball part. Practice starts tomorrow at 11 a.m.

"This day is always weird," Curry said. "There are always a lot of emotions and thoughts on this day because it marks the start of a new year. It's weird, but I know we're excited." ■

Steph Curry drives to the hoop at the Warriors' practice facility in Oakland. (Anda Chu/Staff)

NOVEMBER 7, 2016 • OAKLAND, CALIFORNIA

WARRIORS 116, PELICANS 106

# RECORD BREAKER

## Curry Sets NBA Mark by Making 13 3-Pointers

### By Anthony Slater

Twenty-six feet from the hoop, Kevin Durant stone-walled Stephen Curry's man on a screen. Curry was dodging and weaving and searching for any pocket of air to fire up any semi-reasonable 3-point shot.

Everyone in the building knew what was coming, except, apparently, the Pelicans defense. Anthony Davis, Durant's man, sagged back into the paint, 15 feet from Curry's curl. Durant set a sturdy screen, Draymond Green delivered the pass and Curry, springing open, caught, turned and fired. Bang. It was Curry's 13th made 3, an NBA record for a single game.

During an otherwise underwhelming 116-106 win over the 0-7 Pelicans, Curry's 46-point greatness was needed. And it came just one game after it couldn't be found.

In a blowout loss to the Lakers during the previous game, Curry went 0-of-10 from deep, snapping his NBA record streak of 157 straight games with a made 3-pointer.

"I was hard on myself in practice the last two days," Curry said. "Had pretty good shooting sessions…I've had a new level of focus the last two days trying to get my rhythm back."

Against the Pelicans, it showed. Curry started his new streak early. Less than five minutes in, Durant fired a cross-court transition rocket high and a bit wide. Curry snagged it left-handed like a shortstop snaring a liner up

the middle, landing, firing and hitting with incredible control. Then a contested wing 3 was followed by an open corner look. He had three 3s in the first quarter.

But no other Warrior could find a rhythm from the outside. Andre Iguodala clanged all four of his 3s. Klay Thompson's deep struggles continued. He was 9-of-13 inside the line — nailing a batch of smooth mid-range jumpers — but went 2-of-7 from deep. Outside of Curry, the Warriors went 3-of-18 from 3, many of those far more wide open than many of Curry's 17 attempts.

But the two-time MVP was clearly feeling it. So he started letting them fly from awkward angles amidst a sea of bodies. After fumbling the ball ahead while breaking a double-team in transition, Curry regathered control and, in one motion, let go an off-balance, one-footed leaner with 19 seconds still left on the shot clock. It was an outrageous shot attempt. It went in.

By halftime, he'd hit six. By late in the third quarter, he'd hit eight. But an NBA record didn't seem plausible. Or at least it didn't seem to be on anyone's mind in the building.

Late in the third quarter, Curry pump-faked a 3 and Davis went flying. But the league's scariest shot-blocker couldn't help himself. Davis reached back in search of a no-look swat. Curry caught him, swept his arms through Davis' left hand in a shooting motion. Three free throws were surely coming. But the whistle never blew.

Curry went ballistic. The mouthguard went flying. A

Steph Curry heads down court during the first quarter of his 46-point game. (Jane Tyska/Staff)

technical was called — only the 10th of Curry's career.

"That play was actually a lot of frustration because I'm trying to be coachable," Curry said. "Coach Kerr talked to us about pump-fakes and seeing if we can get guys to fly by. I thought about it in the moment, did it, got AD to fly by and he obviously fouled me...I thought it was a pretty blatant call."

Moments later, still riled up, Curry seemed determined to get back the three points he was just stripped. He dodged through a screen, fired over a contest and popped his ninth, then let out a roar that seemed directed at the nearest referee. Moments later, Curry nailed his 10th, this off one of Golden State's better plays of the night.

Isolated in the mid-post, Kevin Durant pulled the defense his direction. As he backed toward the hoop and they collapsed toward him, Durant fired it cross-court to Thompson. The Pelicans, apparently unaware of who's hot and who's not, ran Thompson off the line and left Curry room to breathe. A swing pass led to his 10th 3 in the final minute of the third quarter.

"That's the first time I thought about (the record)," Curry said.

Then the Warriors otherwise lackluster effort came into effect. Normally in past seasons, if Curry has anywhere near 10 3s, Golden State is smashing the victimized opponent. That allows Curry to sit the fourth and the record stays intact. But the Warriors defense was a step behind in the third quarter, allowing the Pelicans to climb back from a 14-point halftime deficit and no one else could deliver a knockout blow.

So the lead hovered in single digits and Curry returned with 6:48 left. With 3:33 left, he was still at 10 3s. The Pelicans were within five. Then Curry exploded, sealing the game and setting the record with three 3s in a 70-second flurry, capped by that straight-away bullet, set up by the Durant screen and Davis' laziness, which forced a Pelicans timeout.

It surpassed a mark previously set by Donyell Marshall, Kobe Bryant and Curry, who nailed 12 in an overtime win in Oklahoma City last season.

As Curry went to the bench, the crowd erupted into an 'MVP' chant. The jumbotron showed Curry getting mobbed near the bench. Then as he went to take a seat, Durant, next to Curry on the bench, was told of the feat.

"Oh, that's the record?" Durant patted Curry on the head. "Good job, boy." ■

Steph Curry celebrates after hitting his 13th 3-pointer, setting an NBA record for 3-pointers made in a single game. (Jane Tyska/Staff)

DECEMBER 5, 2016 • OAKLAND, CALIFORNIA
WARRIORS 142, PACERS 106

# ZERO TO SIXTY

## Warriors Thompson Fires Away for 60 Points in Just 29 Minutes

### By Anthony Slater

By the time he'd reached the deep corner, inches in front of an erupting Warriors bench, Klay Thompson's night had already gone from lukewarm to hot to scorching to nuclear.

When he's scorching, Thompson searches out shots. When he's nuclear, everyone in the arena searches them out for him, begging Thompson to take anything from anywhere. So he knifed to the corner — spurred on by the crowd — caught, turned and flung an impossible fade from an awkward angle.

It swished through, the three most ridiculous of Thompson's career-high 60 points, done in fewer than three quarters of Golden State's 142-106 blowout of the Pacers.

The fadeaway 3 came midway through the second quarter. Thompson already had 27 points. He'd hit a 3 on the previous two Warriors possessions. You were getting the early sense that one of those Thompson nights was brewing. So did his teammates, who rose in unison, inches from Thompson, as he turned for the deep corner 3.

As Thompson hit it, the entire Warriors' sideline celebrated frantically. JaVale McGee put his hands on his head incredulously. Kevin Durant scurried around the baseline. Stephen Curry, overwhelmed by the moment, first ran toward the scorer's table and then retreated back toward the bench and then past it, sprinting deep into the Warriors' tunnel toward the locker room.

"I ran out of real estate to try to keep my celebration going," Curry said. "I've seen it all from him. When he gets it going, he takes a heat-check turnaround 3 from the corner, heavily contested, and it goes in? Unbelievable."

It was the seminal moment of Thompson's historic night. But it started in uncharacteristic fashion: Inside the paint.

Thompson, of course, is best known for his 3-point sniping, which he displayed on Monday night: eight made 3s on 14 attempts. But what bumped this night from spectacular to legendary was another area of his sometimes neglected scoring repertoire.

Thompson started the night with four reverse layups in the first seven minutes. He cut back door beautifully, leaked out on the fastbreak a pair of times and racked up a ton of early, rare paint points.

"That's what got him going," Kevin Durant said.

Then later in the half, Thompson began a rare parade to the free throw line. He has long struggled to force his way into free points. He entered the night only averaging 2.3 free throw attempts per game, minuscule for a scoring guard. "I think he could average seven or eight per game," Steve Kerr said.

On Monday night, Thompson powered his way to 11

On the way to a 142-106 win over the Pacers, Klay Thompson became the 23rd player to score 60 points in a game. (Jose Carlos Fajardo/Staff)

attempts, one short of a career-high. That included some forceful drives into contact and one particularly crafty play that had Kerr and Curry celebrating on the sideline.

The Warriors coach has long begged Thompson to search contact after his pump-fakes. He has a tendency to side-step and shoot. Once in a while, Kerr wants him to get a guy flying and jump into him, Dwyane Wade style, for an easy whistle.

As he was scorching in the second half, Thompson had what seemed to be an open corner 3. But Monta Ellis sprinted out quickly for the contest. Thompson sensed it, pumped Ellis into the air and jumped into him. Three free throws, three more Thompson points.

"I've been urging him to do that," Kerr said.

"I saw how happy Steve and Mike Brown were after that," Thompson said. "I have to do that more often."

In the third quarter, the Warriors offense revolved around Thompson. But it did so in a differing way than offenses often do when high-volume scorers have it going. Remember Kobe Bryant's 60-point game last April? It was a ton of isolations, dribbling, no-pass possessions as he searched for a shot.

With Thompson, it remains a free-flowing offense, as the ball pings around and Thompson zips everywhere, cutting and running off screens and searching for an open look using the rest of his teammates.

"I don't even know what to say," Kevin Durant said. "Crazy. He probably had the ball in his hands not even two minutes combined the whole game."

Thompson's 58th, 59th and 60th points came with 2:28 left in the third quarter. He lost his defender with a quick fade cut and buried maybe his easiest look of the night. There were still 14 minutes left in the game. There were plenty of points left on the table. But the Warriors led by 38 and Steve Kerr pulled him, saying postgame it was a no-brainer.

"He should've had 80, to be honest," Durant said. "He took 14 threes. The six he missed were probably

open. He missed a free throw, got his layup blocked. We talked about it on the bench. He said he should've had 70. I said you could've had 80-plus. But he had to be perfect to do that."

Thompson became the first player in the shot clock era to finish with 60 points in fewer than 30 minutes. He was the first Warrior in 42 years to score 60. Rick Barry, in 1974, was the last.

And as his historic night came to a close, Thompson left to a rousing ovation, as chants of 'Klay! Klay!' rained down in Oracle. Durant greeted him as he walked off, holding a towel and waving it in front of Thompson like a fan, jokingly trying to cool him off.

In his postgame presser, Thompson called it "something I'll remember forever." And just as he was done with his press conference, Warriors majority owner Joe Lacob entered the room with a rose, walked on stage and presented it to Thompson.

"I'll give this to Rocco," Thompson said, referring to his dog.

Quite a day at the office. The boss was happy. ∎

Klay Thompson shoots a 3-pointer over Indiana's Monta Ellis in the second quarter. Thompson made eight of his 14 attempts from behind the arc. (Jose Carlos Fajardo/Staff)

# 11

## SHOOTING GUARD

# KLAY THOMPSON

## A Legend in the Making

### By Marcus Thompson II • December 6, 2016

The best way to put Klay Thompson into perspective: He can turn basketball royalty into pre-teens having a sugar rush.

He did so, again, scoring 60 points in 29 minutes in a rout of Indiana.

Thompson doesn't have big games. He has events. He has performances that warp basketball reality. He belittles traditional scoring feats by pulling them off with unbecoming ease.

This is becoming Thompson's legacy. An ability to explode at random. A skill so profound it leaves greats baffled.

"I've never seen anything like it," Kevin Durant said. "In 29 minutes? And not even play the fourth quarter? That's unheard of. I mean I've watched Kobe (Bryant) score 80 and 62 in three quarters but to be on a team and be at the game and be on the sideline to watch it, that was crazy."

Durant is the best pure scorer in the NBA. And Thompson's manner of scoring turned him into a giddy kid.

This is why Thompson was not going to be traded. Not because he can be breathtaking. But because he is a critical part of the equation.

Thompson has become legend with these eruptions. Stephen Curry said this latest spectacle topped Thompson's 37 points in a quarter nearly two years ago. He called Thompson's Game 6 performance in the Western Conference Finals "1a" on Thompson's list of historic performances.

While we're at it: the list of Klay Games.

**1. THE GAME OF HIS LIFE**

He scored 41 points at Oklahoma City — with the Warriors facing elimination, with Curry scuffling, with the Warriors trailing and in desperate need of something.

He made 11 threes, a playoff record, and scored 19 in the fourth quarter to leave Durant and the Thunder stunned.

**2. 60**

He only needed 33 shots. Per ESPN's Tom Haberstroh, it only required 11 dribbles.

**3. 37 IN A QUARTER**

That was the last time Thompson turned Oracle into Rucker Park. He turned a close game into a euphoric frenzy with jaw-dropping 3-point shooting. He made nine 3s in the quarter and hit 11 straight shots.

He was in a zone. He just threw it up and it went in.

**4. POSTSEASON BREAKOUT PARTY**

In Game 2 of the 2013 Western Conference semifinals, Thompson scored 34 in three quarters at San Antonio. It was his first "wow" game, coming after the Warriors blew an 18-point fourth quarter lead in Game 1.

The Spurs were bent on stopping Curry, who had 44 in Game 1. Thompson gave a glimpse into the future by making San Antonio pay.

Klay Thompson can put points on the board as explosively as anyone in recent NBA history, as evidenced by his 60 points in 29 minutes against the Pacers in December. (Ray Chavez/Staff)

## 5. 27 IN A QUARTER

**It's small potatoes for Thompson, at this point. He blitzed visiting Phoenix in the third quarter last December.**

**He made nine straight shots, four of them threes, turning a competitive game into a laugher.**

Thompson is becoming a legend for these outbursts. He is less a co-star and more the ruthless right hook in the Warriors' deadly combination. It doesn't always land. But when it does, oh my.

Every opponent has to be gravely concerned about Thompson turning them into a trivia question. And if his own Hall of Fame-bound teammates are blown away, how must opposing defenses feel? Thompson making two straight threes, and the Oracle crowd percolating, has to feel for the defense like the rumble that precedes the avalanche.

The most impressive part is that Thompson does this from the background. Players who blow up like that do so by dominating the ball. Thompson is the rare breed who takes over with the help of his team.

He is a finisher on the best passing team in the league. When the Warriors got Durant, Thompson said he wasn't going to change his game. And he shouldn't. This works because Thompson can take advantage like no other.

He is a top-notch scorer perennially guarded by second and third-notch defenders. He is feasting on open shots, even missed a few wide-open ones Monday that he was still thinking about after.

The Warriors need him to punish teams. And he has developed his game in a way that makes him even more equipped. He is moving off the ball expertly, attacking off the dribble, being smart about when to attack, gets himself into rhythm with his mid-range game.

Durant joked with Thompson that he blew his chance at 80 with his missed layups and bricked threes.

"I hate when I miss a wide-open corner three. That's like a layup to a shooter," Thompson said. "All of the best shooters to ever play this game are all big time perfectionists as players. Me, Steph and Kevin are no different. I just want to make every shot."

Because he downs these things, his threat is nearly as impactful as his production. The fact that he can launch into these Twilight Zone moments is etched into the mind of every team the Warriors play.

And when his career is over, he will go down as one of those players who is most known for impressing his colleagues.

There is a list of all-time greats fans swoon over. And then there is the list that all-time greats swoon over. Those players that aren't marketed to the masses like the top tier superstars, but those who played against them are still shaking their heads 20 years later. Their impact isn't best expressed by their resume, but by their ability to make the best marvel.

Earl "The Pearl" Monroe. Bernard King. Elvin Hayes. Mitch Richmond. Kevin Johnson. Rod Strickland. Tracy McGrady. Gilbert Arenas.

Thompson will be like them. Everyone will remember Curry, Durant, LeBron James, Anthony Davis and James Harden from this era. But those players will be the ones to say "Don't forget about Klay."

The highlight of the night underscored how Thompson boggles the best.

It looked like a move straight from the 80s video game "Double Dribble." Thompson caught the pass facing the crowd and moving towards the baseline. In one graceful motion, Thompson caught it, turned and fired — still drifting in the air — and drilled the 3-pointer over Monta Ellis' best defense of the night. He landed out of bounds.

Curry, on the bench, couldn't contain himself. He ran towards halfcourt, then back toward the bench, leaping into his teammates. He then weaved through his celebrating teammates and ran into the tunnel and out of sight.

Thompson's craziness had the two-time MVP looking like a 7-year-old who desperately had to pee.

"That's a feat that I would put money on to probably never be touched ever again in the history of basketball. It's unbelievable," Curry said of Klay's 60 points in fewer than 30 minutes. "We have to be able to enjoy those historical performances. That's what the game is all about." ▪

Thompson tends to fly under the radar among the star-studded Warriors, but his scoring and perimeter defense are indispensable to the team's identity. (Nhat V. Meyer/Staff)

## HEAD COACH

# STEVE KERR

## Coach Is Unafraid to Champion Political Issues

By Anthony Slater • February 19, 2017

The NBA world has descended upon New Orleans this weekend for the All-Star Game. Twenty-four players comprise the two rosters. Four of the weekend's biggest names are Warriors: Stephen Curry, Kevin Durant, Draymond Green and Klay Thompson.

But the team's private jet brought along another of the league's biggest newsmakers: Steve Kerr, the Western Conference coach, who has emerged as a leading voice on social issues during one of the most polarizing times in the country's history.

Within the past year, Kerr has publicly addressed gun control, Colin Kaepernick's national anthem protest, medical marijuana, President Donald Trump's rhetoric and most recently Trump's travel ban on seven Muslim-majority countries.

"We have a president who has no regard for compassion or empathy, in the most important leadership position in the world," Kerr said in an exclusive interview this week. "The most important thing in being a leader — as a parent, a teacher, a coach — is dignity for the position you are in, empathy for others. You're trying to help people. And it feels like we're in a time where our leader is just ridiculing constantly — on Twitter, whether it's making fun of a handicapped person, or tweeting about how horrible *Saturday Night Live* is, the failing *New York Times*, casting the media as the opposition.

"This is not leadership. And I think people realize that. It should not matter if you are a conservative or a liberal. It's about leadership, it's about compassion and dignity and character and treating people the right way.

That's leadership. It's terrifying we have someone in office who espouses none of that."

In a coaching profession that is traditionally all sports all the time — where consumers go to escape the real world and aligned fan bases have split political views — why is Kerr so willing to speak his mind on controversial topics? The answer is found in a perfect storm of factors: Kerr is with the right team in the right league and the right market. But mostly he is the right man.

"Coach Kerr has been through so much in his life personally," said Durant. "He realizes, checks the pulse of our country and our world. He knows exactly what he's talking about. He's so informed and intelligent when it comes to topics, social issues. He gets it and a lot of coaches don't."

Kerr, 51, was born in Lebanon. He spent much of his childhood either in Los Angeles or traveling throughout the Middle East. His father, Malcolm, was a decorated academic who became the chairman of the Department of Political Sciences at UCLA and later the president of the American University of Beirut.

Kerr's first memories of political conversations happened at the dinner table when he was 7. His parents would regularly discuss the 1972 presidential race between Richard Nixon and George McGovern. The Vietnam War was going on. The evening news was always on.

"We talked a lot about world politics," Kerr said. "Late '70s, I was 13, 14, started reading about stuff. That was a pretty important time — the peace process, Camp David, President Carter getting Begin and Sadat together."

Malcolm Kerr was shot and killed in 1984 outside his campus office in Beirut in an act of terrorism. Steve

Warriors players listen to head coach Steve Kerr during a timeout. (Jose Carlos Fajardo/Staff)

Kerr was 18. The tragedy is at the root of his passion about gun control and more recently Trump's travel ban, something he sees as a "shocking" and "horrible" idea.

"I would just say that as someone whose family member was a victim of terrorism, having lost my father, if we're trying to combat terrorism by banishing people from coming to this country, it's really going against what the principles of what our country's about and creating fear," Kerr said after a game in Portland two weeks ago. "If anything, we could be breeding anger and terror and so I'm completely against what's happening."

Kerr has developed a simple strategy: If he's versed and he's passionate and he's asked about a subject, he'll answer. If he's not, he won't. He doesn't avoid controversies, but he tries not to seek them out. He has declined several recent invites from CNN and other political shows to be a panelist or tell his story.

"I think you should only say something if you're comfortable saying it, " Kerr said. "There could be plenty of reasons why people would not be comfortable — whether it's their personal beliefs. I know there are certain things I would never talk about because I don't know about them."

Much like his childhood, Kerr had a unique, informed NBA upbringing, playing under two of the league's greatest, most outspoken coaches: Phil Jackson and Gregg Popovich. Jackson used to gather his Chicago Bulls teams for open forums.

"I remember Phil one time asked our team: 'How many of you own guns?'" Kerr said. "'How many of you know that you're more likely to have a death in your home with a gun than without a gun?'"

In Popovich, the coach of the San Antonio Spurs, Kerr found a mentor.

"He was in the military, went to the Air Force Academy, served his country," Kerr said. "From a worldview, Russian major, studied Eastern Europe. Every time you go into his office, CNN is on, not *SportsCenter*."

While playing under Popovich for the Spurs, Kerr caused his first public controversy. It came after the 9/11 attacks. Kerr opposed the Iraq War. "Being in Texas, it wasn't the most popular stance," he said.

There were several letters to the editor at the local paper calling him unpatriotic. Kerr held his ground.

"I think there's a big difference in supporting the military and protesting the war," Kerr said. "I don't think those are mutually exclusive. If anything, people who protested that war were actually being much more patriotic than people who were fervently waving the flag without giving the war much thought. The damage that's done, the lives that were lost, the families that were forever changed. People need to stop and think, while they're waving the flag and chanting U-S-A, is the war just?"

Kerr's voice has grown stronger for reasons outside himself. One is job security.

As Ron Adams, his lead assistant coach, said: "When you start a new job, you don't just come in and do that. But once you win a championship, people take notice."

Then there's the market and league — the Bay Area and NBA — which provide a left-leaning safe haven. Kerr has seen plenty of blowback for his comments but says the criticism has all been online. In person, he says, there has been only gratitude for speaking out.

"When I was in the NBA (as a player), there were plenty of conservatives in the locker room, usually having to do with just taxes," Kerr said. "Fiscal conservatives. Which makes sense. Vote for one guy and you save a lot more money. So there were plenty of guys who voted Republican. Nowadays I think there are very few. But it's almost 100 percent based on social justice. Whether it's police killings that players can now look at on their phone or immigration laws that affect 100 foreign players in the league or the tone of racism that's gone on in this recent campaign, you have a lot more guys who are not only leaning to the left, but much more willing to speak up."

The Warriors have a few: Green, Andre Iguodala, David West, even Curry recently. Kerr has gathered the team for occasional open forums, but it's mostly just personal conversations.

Recently, Kerr and West engaged in a discussion about Betsy DeVos' nomination for the U.S. secretary of education.

"It's refreshing, honestly, to have someone so engaged with what's going on in our world, who knows that things going on outside this NBA bubble can clearly affect folks inside the bubble," West said.

To Kerr, it's just his way of life.

"What we're seeing right now, there's a lot of chaos, a lot of turmoil," he said. "I think it's important we don't just sit back and idly let all these things happen." ■

After sitting out due to back-related medical issues, Steve Kerr returned to coach his team for Game 2 of the NBA Finals. (Dan Honda/Staff)

FEBRUARY 11, 2017 • OKLAHOMA CITY, OKLAHOMA
WARRIORS 130, THUNDER 114

# SO SWEET

## Kevin Durant Takes OKC's Best Shot, Still Comes Out on Top

### By Marcus Thompson II

There were cupcakes everywhere, with sprinkles made of venom. The Midwestern charm and Southern hospitality that usually intersect here was replaced with good ol' fashioned rage.

The disdain for Kevin Durant was palpable. It was also legible. Signs around the arena attacked his character, questioned his fortitude and loyalty. They exalted Russell Westbrook, the superstar who stayed, and jeered the former MVP with all their might. It was a ceremony of disownership.

But in the end, Durant absorbed all their anger. He weathered their insults, swallowed their verbal attacks, endured their taunts. He consumed everything OKC threw at him, used it as power, and then unleashed it on them.

It was arguably the most intense regular season blowout in NBA history, a 130-114 Warriors road win. And Durant emerged the star, leading the Warriors with 34 points and nine rebounds. He finally dished it back to Westbrook. He punched back at Oklahoma.

For at least a week, Durant waded through the hype, struggling to keep his emotions and focus in check as his return neared. And when he arrived, the mood of the arena justified his angst.

They didn't just boo him. They took pleasure in ridiculing him. Kids and adults, who once deemed him their favorite, brazenly mocked him. Some thought fans should cheer Durant, appreciate the near decade he devoted to them. But it was clear they deemed him no longer worthy of their affection.

They blew up old tweets of Durant proclaiming his love for Oklahoma City and his desire to never leave. Others wore shirts that called him a coward, but it was spelled with a K and his initials bookending the insult were highlighted. One kid came dressed up in a cupcake costume with Durant's number on it.

The cupcake thing stems from Durant's time with the Thunder. Kendrick Perkins, their center back then, referred to anything soft as "cupcake." When Durant announced he was signing with the Warriors, Westbrook posted a picture of a cupcake on Instagram.

When the game began, Durant looked bothered, just as he has the last few games. He made his first shot but wound up 2-for-8 in the first quarter after forcing most of his looks. Every time he touched the ball, he was booed. Every mistake he made was celebrated.

But in the middle of the game, Durant was triggered. He'd been playing it cool as this game approached, trying to say the right things, be positive and take the high road. But he decided to stop playing nice.

In the third quarter, Westbrook drove the lane for a layup and Durant tried to block it. He was unsuccessful, but on the way down court he barked about it being an

Amid taunts and boos from Oklahoma City fans, Kevin Durant dunks over Thunder guard Anthony Morrow for two of his 34 points. (AP Images)

offensive foul to Westbrook, who complained to the ref about not getting the foul call. Westbrook barked back.

It was on.

The two started jawing at each other. During a timeout, it escalated beyond inaudible whispers in passing. They were full-on trash talking.

Westbrook shouted, "I'm coming."

Durant: "You're losing."

Westbrook again: "I'm coming."

Durant shrugged. "So what."

The civility was over. Durant had exited the high road. And now he was the one with a vengeance. His teammates enjoyed it.

"Absolutely," Shaun Livingston said. "I loved it."

Durant went on a mission to shut up Westbrook, who has been dissing Durant since July 4. To shut up his former teammates, whom he thought were taking cheap elbows and shoves on him. To shut up the thousands of fans, hundreds of thousands in Oklahoma City, whose love for him was not unconditional.

Durant scored 19 points in the second half. He got a technical foul for jawing and colliding with Thunder forward Andre Roberson. He went back and forth with Westbrook, who got hot and turned the game into a Rucker Park-style showdown.

This was Durant with a chip on his shoulder, with edge. This was Durant setting aside his thoughtfulness and humanity, allowing himself to be governed by the merciless baller from D.C. inside him. He had taken all he could take.

He punctuated his performance with Westbrook defending him. Standing near the left hash mark, Durant rose up and shot over Westbrook from 28 feet away. And when the net splashed, he stood there and stared at the Thunder point guard.

This time, it was Durant taunting Westbrook.

Here is the major difference in their approach, highlighted in the exchange with Westbrook: Durant is not consumed by these 1-on-1 battles. He doesn't seem to believe in the model that prevented him from winning a title with the Thunder, the same style of play that has Westbrook revered.

Westbrook is beloved because he put Oklahoma on his shoulders, and he attacks the league with a me-against-the-world ferocity.

Notice he said "I'm coming."

Durant's retort, is in essence, "We're coming."

Because he also got 26 points and nine assists from Stephen Curry, another 26 from Klay Thompson. While Durant rested, the Warriors second unit took over the game.

Durant walked into one of the toughest environments in recent memory. When the smoke cleared and the chanting stopped, he was still standing. And he wasn't alone. He thrived despite the hatred because he is on a loaded squad that values the collective.

After the game, Curry and Green dished back some of the ridicule the Thunder fans threw at Durant. Security guards hustled up some of the cupcake T-shirts fans were wearing for the Warriors players. Curry and Green wore theirs during their postgame interviews.

Icing on the cupcake. ∎

Russell Westbrook jaws with his former teammate Kevin Durant, who got the upper hand with the Warriors' 130-114 victory. (AP Images)

# 9

## SMALL FORWARD

# ANDRE IGUODALA

## Springy Andre Iguodala Gives Warriors a Boost

### By Marcus Thompson II • March 27, 2017

A simple hesitation move froze the entire Memphis defense. The pause created an opening and Andre Iguodala sliced through it, soaring for a tomahawk dunk.

Iguodala's hesitations normally prevent explosive dunks, not create them. He's known to drive and look for the pass, avoiding the rim like a tough conversation. But in the 106-94 win over the Grizzlies, Iguodala was a slashing, bouncing scorer. He recorded 20 points, seven rebounds, four assists and two steals in 32 minutes off the bench.

But this wasn't a one-night flash. The 33-year-old has been springy for a while now. He's been driving the lane with zeal, posting up smaller guards like he is insulted by their defense. And when he's near the rim, he's looking to throw it down.

It's late March. The season is 70 games old. Why is the 13-year veteran looking so fresh this time of year?

"Yoga and cryotherapy," Iguodala said. "And salt floating."

Outside of seeing Kevin Durant back in uniform, the most welcomed sight for Warriors fans has to be Iguodala playing like a 25-year-old.

Since Durant got hurt, Iguodala's production has ticked up noticeably. He averaged 11.6 points on 61.8 percent shooting in March, easily his best month of the season.

He is still the secret weapon, the special ingredient in the Warriors' high-powered engine. Iguodala carving up defenses and locked on to opposing stars is the best indicator of the Warriors' championship potential. Because if he's playing well, on top of the four All-Stars, that typically means the Warriors are unstoppable.

"He's been fantastic," coach Steve Kerr said. "He looks incredibly athletic, bouncy and fresh. He's a pro. The guy just knows how to take care of his body. I think he's done a great job of stepping up in KD's absence and recognizing what we need from him. He's been brilliant."

He has already eclipsed last season's minutes total. Yet Iguodala is getting stronger.

Can it really be 7:30 am yoga sessions a few times a week? He gets cryotherapy — a recovery method using cold temperatures — every home game. He's been hitting the spa to float in epsom salt more frequently.

Is that why he leads the Warriors in field goal percentage since Durant went down? Is that why he is shooting 44 percent from 3 in that span?

If it is, the Warriors can only hope he continues. An aggressive Iguodala on offense is a boon to the Warriors' bench and a pressure-release for the starters.

A sure starter on most other teams in the league, sixth man Andre Iguodala shoots from the perimeter during the Warriors' Game 2 victory in the NBA Finals. (Ray Chavez/Staff)

He is a demoralizer, gut punches for a defense that has to work incredibly hard to contain Durant, Stephen Curry and Klay Thompson.

Iguodala attacking and making plays is an immediate jolt, especially when the Warriors are struggling. And after the worst stretch in the Kerr era, Iguodala's impact was desperately needed.

"He brings so much energy off the bench with all sorts of different lineups," Curry said. "His ability is always evident. It shows up all across the stat sheet. He's aggressive with scoring and knocking down shots. Playing inspired basketball, it's unbelievable. We feed off of his energy when we see him get a rebound, get a steal, push up the court, make a crazy inside-out dribble and finish at the rim, knock down open threes, play make for other guys. It's fun to watch. He always says, 'Y'all forget that I can play basketball, too.' But we don't forget that and we love to see it."

If this is the Iguodala the Warriors can expect in the playoffs, they will be tough to beat. When Durant returns from injury, the load will lighten for Iguodala. But if the confidence he's built, and the fresh legs he's exhibiting, sticks around for the postseason, it solves a lot of the issues the Warriors have off the bench.

If this is the Iguodala the Warriors can expect in the playoffs, they should probably start getting used to life without him. A productive postseason is sure to drive the price up for the pending free agent.

Since they have to sign Durant and Curry, the Warriors won't have much money to offer their sixth man. Which means if Iguodala gets a lucrative deal elsewhere, he'd be forced to choose between one last big pay day and offering a discount to the franchise with which he's reinvented himself.

That sounds like something to ponder in the salt float. ■

Always energetic, Andre Iguodala shadowboxes prior to Game 4 of the Western Conference Finals. (Jose Carlos Fajardo/Staff)

# 23

## POWER FORWARD

# DRAYMOND GREEN

### Going Green, Seeing Red

By Carl Steward • April 16, 2017

The list of things most NBA experts believe could deny the Warriors a second championship in three years is short.

A major injury. Overconfidence that leads to sloppy play. A fluky offensive cold streak.

Then there's that nagging notion lingering from last postseason: That their defensive dynamo and all-around emotional engine could blow a gasket at any time.

Whether Draymond Green likes it or not, it's a real concern for many Warriors fans. It's a talking point in the national media, and even more so on social media.

Can Draymond play on the edge without going over it?

Intuitive person that he is, Green's protective shields go up at the mere hint of the topic. Asked point-blank if he feels he's harnessed his emotions much better this year, he answered, "Yeah, I think so, but…"

But?

"But we act like it's been a problem the whole time," he said. "We won a championship and lost in a Game 7. So it couldn't have been too bad. That's the 'but.' "

But … it won't stop people's vivid recollections of Game 4 of last year's NBA Finals, and Green's subsequent Game 5 suspension that helped the Cleveland Cavaliers get back into the series and eventually win it.

Green's college coach at Michigan State, Tom Izzo, reflected on the Game 4 LeBron James step-over move that resulted in the suspension and said it was an incident that his former player and the Warriors needed to learn

from the hard way. Whether Green was baited into retaliation or not, Izzo believes a steep price was paid.

"I'm not saying (James) did it on purpose, because nobody should step over anybody at any level," Izzo said. "I thought it was kind of a weak technical call myself. But do I think it had an impact on the game? I definitely do. Draymond is involved in so many winning plays both offensively and defensively, it's harder to lose him than any player on that team. That doesn't mean he's the best player, but he might be the best winner.

"He's so valuable to the team that some of that stuff as far as technicals, he's got to figure out a way not to let it happen. I still feel that way."

Green had another fabulous All-Star season. He led the league in steals. He's a good bet to win NBA Defensive Player of the Year. He was second in assists behind James among forwards. Nobody his size had remotely as many blocked shots. And his team finished the regular season 67-15.

Detractors, however, point to his 15 technical fouls, tied for second-most in the league behind DeMarcus Cousins and one short of the automatic suspension limit, and two flagrant fouls. They bring up his on-court scolding of Kevin Durant and a couple of notable sideline clashes with coach Steve Kerr.

For his part, however, Kerr maintained Green has exhibited tremendous emotional growth this season in spite of those occasional boil-over moments in the heat of battle.

Draymond Green celebrates his 3-point basket in the first quarter of the Warriors' blowout victory in Game 2 of the Western Conference Finals (Nhat V. Meyer/Staff)

"He picks his spots now, when to talk and when to back off, which makes his words more effective," Kerr said. "I just think he's gotten wiser. Maybe fatherhood helped a little bit, too, and the experiences of what he's gone through in his young career."

To be sure, Green has no shortage of people looking out for his best interests with support and advice. Izzo, who still talks or texts with him multiple times a week, loves him like a son. There's Luke Walton, the former Warriors assistant coach and confidant, who still talks to him regularly. There's Kerr, of course. And no one should forget one of his toughest critics — his mother, Mary Babers-Green — who always has her son's ear.

But Green picked up an important new ally and unofficial guardian angel this season with the Warriors' signing of 14-year veteran big man David West. Green acknowledges West has been a sage voice for him in a lot of areas, including how to best apply his emotional effervescence.

"He's helped me a lot, talked to me a lot about channeling that," Green said. "Knowing when to use that, knowing how not to let it work against me. He's helped me with everything — emotionally, leadership-wise, seeing different things with the game. He's extremely smart."

Added Kerr regarding West, "David has provided so much leadership, and particularly for Draymond. He's just a voice of reason. There have been times when Draymond has gotten pretty emotional and David has pulled him aside and calmed him down by saying something much more valuable than anything I could say or any of the coaches could say."

West fully understands Green must play with a high emotional intensity to get the most out of his skill set.

"I don't think he's as effective if he's not pushing that line," West said. "I just talk to him about letting his mind get him through it. Sometimes when you get emotional, your thoughts become scattered and you're all over the place. You just have to know time and place. You don't want to take that emotion away, though, because it's what makes him unique.

"It's just about him having that control, knowing when to rev it up, pull it back. I've tried to help him snap out of it a few times. I think sometimes he gets so gone, you have to be able to pull him back."

Another veteran player who is no stranger to driving himself with emotional play, the Lakers' Metta World Peace, watches and admires Green from afar and hopes he learned from last year's suspension and warned that other players will do whatever is necessary — even bait a high-emotion player — to get under their skin.

Did LeBron?

"No, that was all (Green's) fault. He made a mistake, but everybody makes mistakes," World Peace said. "He has to learn from it and I think he did. He knows he can't win a title sitting in the locker room on a suspension. He has been the type of player you could bait, but I think he's smart enough now not to take the bait. He's very intelligent."

World Peace doesn't worry about Green's technical count.

"He gets technical fouls, but you're allowed one tech before you get ejected," he said. "Sometimes you can take a tech that'll change the game. Sometimes his techs look very calculated, and he's doing it for the right reasons. They get his team into it."

They still drive Izzo nuts, though. The coach said he was watching a game last week on TV where Green was jawing at a ref and he started yelling, "Don't do it! Don't do it!" He promptly sent him admonishing texts that he'd read after the game.

Izzo added that he has talked with Kerr and Warriors general manager Bob Myers many times about Green. He thought it was a great thing that Myers sat with Draymond in an A's suite during Game 5 last year to support him during the suspension. In short, he knows the Warriors realize the rewards of his play far outweigh the risks of his temper.

"You have to understand Draymond to deal with it," Izzo said. "He did that here (at Michigan State) where he would get angry and upset. Does he once in a while get carried away? Sure. But people who do that, wear their emotions on their sleeve, let me tell you, I've made mistakes myself. But at least when people come to a game, they know it matters to me. I always know it matters to Draymond. Is that worth a little B.S. once in a while? Damn right it is." ■

Despite being fouled by LeBron James, Draymond Green scores two of his 12 points in Game 1 of the NBA Finals. (Jose Carlos Fajardo/Staff)

## ASSISTANT COACH

# MIKE BROWN

## Harley Man Got Career in Gear with Popovich Assist

By Anthony Slater • May 14, 2017

A year ago around this time, Steve Kerr was in the market for a new lead assistant and Mike Brown was a target. But before Kerr called Brown, he called San Antonio Spurs coach Gregg Popovich.

Brown was hanging around the Spurs some. Popovich was the mutual connection. Among Kerr's questions for Popovich: Is Brown really ready to dive back into coaching full-time?

"Pop got off the phone and told me Steve may call," Brown said. "Then he told me: 'If he does and he offers you the job, you better take it! You've been out long enough.'"

With Popovich serving as the middle man, the connection turned into a partnership that turned into a path, weaving to this unlikely moment just a year later: Brown filling in as head coach for the ailing Kerr, readying his Warriors to face Popovich's Spurs in the West Finals. The reward: a likely chance to square up, on the sport's biggest stage, with a Cleveland franchise that has fired Brown twice this decade. What a time to be Mike Brown.

But three days before one of the most stressful stretches of his professional life, Brown seems anything but stressed as he pulls up to a Peet's Coffee on the north side of Oakland, wearing a plaid shirt that matches his beige green Harley. He wrestles it into a parking spot, greets a few fans, unstraps his matte black helmet, plants himself on a stool near the window and, for the next 90 minutes, gazes toward the hills as he recaps the past three years of his life — a period of revitalization thanks to an NBA sabbatical, his two sons, a motorcycle, Popovich and Kerr.

"My perspective on life and work has changed dramatically," he says.

Brown was hired by the Cavaliers, for a second time, in late April of 2013. Brown was fired in early May of 2014, less than 13 months into a five-year, $20 million deal. He sensed it was coming.

Around the All-Star break, owner Dan Gilbert axed general manager Chris Grant, his friend and biggest ally in the organization. "That kind of shook me," Brown said. David Griffin was hired to replace Grant. "We didn't see eye to eye," Brown said.

He'd been in the business long enough. He knew he was next. Two months later, he was. So there Brown sat in May of 2014, holed up in the huge house he'd just purchased, his life suddenly in an unfamiliar place.

### BASKETBALL LIFER

Brown, 47, played basketball through college and went right into coaching after that. He was a video guy at 22, an assistant by 27 and a head coach by 35. "There are a lot of smart people out there," Brown said. "The only thing I had control over was working harder than the next guy."

So that's what his life became: basketball, basketball, basketball and family, not much else. Brown met his eventual wife, Carolyn, at 23. They had their first son, Elijah, when Mike was 25 and their second son, Cameron, when Mike was 27. They all grew up together in the NBA world.

But by May of 2014, his two boys had entered independent stages. Elijah was in his second year of college, having transferred from Butler to New Mexico

Mike Brown confers with head coach Steve Kerr during Game 2 against the Cleveland Cavaliers. (Nhat V. Meyer/Staff)

because Brad Stevens left for the NBA. Cameron was in his last year of high school, soon setting off for Cincinnati. And in January of 2015, Mike and his wife divorced.

Forever, he was the dad with the young kids and the cool job that kept him extremely busy. Life was frantic. Now he was the dad with too much free time and a disappearing list of responsibilities. Life became mellow.

"I was basically just trying to find myself away from basketball," Brown said. "I tried expanding my horizons."

He exercised more to keep from going stir-crazy. He grabbed some tools and helped keep the local high school football field in playing shape. He tried to dig into a few leadership books. "But I'm not a reader," Brown said.

## CYCLE TIME

Still in a search of a hobby, Brown hopped on his motorcycle. It became his release. Sometimes twice a week, he'd rev it up from his Cleveland home and take the two-hour round trip across the south shore of Lake Erie toward Cedar Point's famous theme park, blasting Beastie Boys or whatever would calm him as he collected his thoughts on Ohio's open road.

Year 1 of his sabbatical ended and basketball still hadn't drawn him back. Teams called, offering assistant jobs, but nothing excited him. The business side of things had scarred him, but Brown maintains he never got bitter. He knows how fortunate he's been professionally. "I'm pretty good at moving on," he said.

But both his boys were now off at college, his ex-wife was out of the house and, just down the road, LeBron James had returned and the Cavaliers had bolted back to prominence, overtaking the region. It was time to hit restart and get out of Cleveland.

So for Year 2 of the sabbatical, Brown stationed himself in a small apartment in Albuquerque, just down the road from the University of New Mexico, where his son, after a redshirt transfer season, was preparing to star as the school's high-scoring wing.

## CALL FROM POPOVICH

But about two months before the college season, Gregg Popovich called with an invite: Come to the Spurs' annual coach's meeting in Newport Beach. Brown did. And while there, Popovich had an open offer: Any time he wanted to be around the Spurs during the upcoming season, he could. Just call Popovich's secretary and set it up.

"Extremely important," Brown said. "I was feeling like I wanted to get back in, but I wasn't quite there yet. So to be able to do it this way, it was unbelievable. I couldn't have asked for a better situation, a better guy, a better organization at the time to be able to do that with."

It allowed him to sort his priorities exactly how he wanted. When New Mexico was playing, Brown was there to see Elijah — home or road. He went to 31 of their 32 games that season, only missing the game at UNLV because UNLV had just fired its coach and rumors were floating that Brown may be the next guy. "Missed that one on purpose," he said.

But the college season is shorter and spread out. So any time he had the NBA itch, Brown would meet up with the Spurs for days at a time. He'd stay at Danny Ferry's vacant house in Alamo Heights, where Brown left a vehicle and clothes. Ferry moved to Atlanta for the Hawks' GM job years earlier, but never sold his home. Brown slept in Ferry's son's old room.

"Every time I go to sleep, I'm in this Spiderman bed with this Spiderman fathead looking over me," Brown laughed. "Yeah, life was different."

## ALL ACCESS

Popovich gave him unobstructed access to everything. He went to practices when he wanted and took part in every coaching meeting — pregame, halftime, postgame — during the "40 or 50" games he attended.

Brown was an assistant with the Spurs 14 years earlier, back in the early 2000s, when Popovich was younger and sterner, in some ways forming Brown's regimented approach. Back then, Brown and now Hawks coach Mike Budenholzer split up the scouting reports. They had to fax it to Popovich by 7 p.m. the night before the game. Like a high school teacher shredding a rough draft, Popovich layered through them in red ink before sending it back for corrections.

"He used to put notes on it if the spelling was

Mike Brown has a laugh while addressing the media following Game 2 of the Western Conference finals against the San Antonio Spurs. Brown took over head coaching duties during Steve Kerr's medical leave of absence. (Jose Carlos Fajardo/Staff)

incorrect, if the grammar was off," Brown said.

Fourteen years later, Brown watched as a more tranquil Popovich allowed his assistants to bring the reports in the morning, trusting his own immense knowledge of the league and reading over it just before addressing the team. "There are a lot of things he just let go easier," Brown said.

It was an example Brown would store in his back pocket for his next job, a realization that, hmm, coaches can evolve and alter their approach over time.

Early this season, Kerr sent Brown to a far court to work with a group of Warriors on some offensive sets. He rounded them up — this collection of Hall of Fame talents and self-sufficient veterans — and began to methodically take them through the drill.

"I'm very structured. 'We're going from Point A to Point B to Point C,'" Brown said. "But that's not how they play. That's not how they learn either. I started doing that stuff and — I've been around a bit — so I know and feel if something's not right. Now they were respectful, but I could feel right away they're like we don't need you to hold our hands and walk us through this. We just need a little direction and once in a while, if we're not doing the right way, say something."

## LEARNING THE WARRIOR WAY

Brown backed off. He was starting to understand the vibe. He began to meld into the organization's culture, while still picking his spots to teach. Maybe one day down the road, if he returned to the top seat, he'd bring some of this with him.

Then Kerr's lingering health issues worsened and the coach was forced off the sidelines. Boom! Welcome to your test run, Mike Brown 2.0. Your first objective: Don't allow the Warriors — a notoriously unfocused Game 3 team (2-6 the past two years) — let up with a 2-0 lead in Portland. What happens? They fall behind 13 at half and 17 in the third quarter.

Earlier in his coaching career, when LeBron was a pup and Brown was still in his 30s, he'd get so tense on the sidelines, stressing in key moments. A veteran, he thinks it was Eric Snow, told him: "You have to watch how you react to things and your facial expressions. Because if they're the wrong way or not positive, it can bring us down as a team, as a group."

"I tried to take it to heart," Brown said. "But as a young head coach, experiencing things for the first time, I couldn't always control that."

But here he was in Portland, a truly important moment in his career, remaining calm on the sidelines during a rough patch. The Warriors stampeded back for a win. After the game, Draymond Green called Brown the game's "MVP." Klay Thompson said "we appreciated his composure." Thinking back to Snow's advice, Brown was just proud of the personal growth he felt.

"I've relied on my past experience as a head coach," Brown said. "But also, a lot of what came into play was what I learned this season, how Steve handles things."

A couple weeks later, Kerr remains out, which means Brown remains the leading man. The Warriors are 6-0 with him in charge. The adjustment has gone smoothly. But things are about to heat up. He's currently staring down the barrel of two challenging, familiar tasks: a showdown with Popovich's Spurs before a potential Finals date with LeBron and the ghosts of Cleveland past.

## NATURE GUY

How stressed is Brown? Meh. He knows what kind of talent he's lugging around. He'd rather talk about his recent trip into the Oakland Hills. Brown called the Bay Area his favorite place he's ever lived because he can hop on his motorcycle and "10 minutes later, you're in a completely different world."

Brown revved the Harley up, left downtown and climbed Lake Chabot road near Castro Valley. Before long, he was up in the hills, stunned by the mix of forestry and creeks, lakes and wildlife. He had to show somebody. So he hopped off his bike, started snapping pictures with his iPhone to text friends and then thought to himself, wait: "I'm not a picture guy. I'm not a nature guy."

Correction: The old Mike Brown wasn't. The new one seems to be. ■

Stephen Curry listens to Mike Brown during a time out against the Utah Jazz. (Nhat V. Meyer/Staff)

# 35
## SMALL FORWARD

# KEVIN DURANT

### Singular Focus

By Tim Kawakami • May 24, 2017

The three of them sat quietly and contentedly side by side, lined up in the Warriors' locker room late Monday night, no need for words at this moment.

It was Draymond Green at one locker, the large and newly claimed Western Conference finals trophy taking up the next one, and Kevin Durant sitting one more spot over — with all three calmly soaking in the Warriors' just completed sweep of the San Antonio Spurs and looking ready for so much more.

You could feel that this was an important but incomplete scene, signifying the realization of something special — a historic 12-0 start to the playoffs and a third straight berth in the NBA Finals — and of course the beginning of the preparation for the last and greatest step.

I asked Durant: Do you feel like this right here is a fulfillment of almost everything you hoped to achieve by signing with the Warriors last summer?

"I just wanted to come and enjoy this atmosphere, enjoy this culture," Durant said, glancing to Green and the rest of his teammates.

"All I was worried about was every single day, how can I be the best player I can be, how can I leave my imprint on these guys; and I think I did a great job of that."

Yes, all of that has come true, through Monday's series-clinching victory over San Antonio, when Durant and Stephen Curry took turns decimating the Spurs

defense in the second half, just the way you might figure two MVPs would do.

Leaving permanent imprints on the West playoffs.

All of this has happened about as smoothly as anything of this magnitude could. Factoring in a few injuries to Durant and also the Warriors indefinitely losing coach Steve Kerr two games into the postseason, the Warriors' 12-0 run has been a consummate performance.

For Durant, who was criticized so harshly for his decision to leave Oklahoma City and join the Warriors, and who is still hearing criticism about it even now, 10 months later, the new era started with that meeting with Curry, Green, Klay Thompson and Andre Iguodala in The Hamptons.

And from there, it all connects to their shot at the NBA Finals starting June 1 against either Cleveland or Boston, and yes, they hope it's Cleveland.

Durant knows that it will all be called a failure — and probably will feel like one — if the Warriors don't win the championship next month. Just as last season's record-breaking 73-victory campaign was scarred by the Game 7 loss to Cleveland.

But Durant says the joy of this season, and the cumulative march to this point, has been the proof of his decision.

"You know the big goal, but it's definitely amazing to get here, to grind with this team all year," Durant said.

Kevin Durant (35) drives against LeBron James (23) in Game 1 of the NBA Finals. Durant and James previously met in the Finals in 2012, as members of the Thunder and Heat respectively. (Nhat V. Meyer/Staff)

"We didn't really talk about a championship all season — it was just always about every single day playing good basketball. And it led us here.

"Definitely a great checkpoint and we want to continue to keep going."

This isn't Durant's first deep trip into the postseason — his Thunder team almost beat the Warriors in last year's Western Conference finals, which foreshadowed the Warriors' eventual loss to Cleveland in the Finals; and also, in 2012, when he was just 23, his young Thunder team lost in the Finals to LeBron James' Miami Heat team.

So both Durant and his Warriors teammates have some extreme interest in playing — and beating — LeBron in the 2017 Finals.

"Obviously happy for him to be sharing this moment with him after all he's gone through with joining the squad and leaving OKC," Green said at the postgame podium of Durant.

"To be headed to the NBA Finals is a great way to combat all that talk. To win it would be even better. He doesn't seem like he's overjoyed or anything like that. Excited to be headed to The Finals, but at the same time, he knows.

"He didn't make the decision he made to go to the Finals. He made the decision he made, No. 1, for his own life and where he was at in his life and what he wanted to do, but also to win a championship. To go win."

Could the Warriors have gotten through the West without Durant? Possibly. But that's not the issue. The point is that they are measurably better with Durant worked in as a core piece of this, and that is what the Warriors are showing the world in these playoffs.

Now they have him for the Finals, presumably against Cleveland, which does seem rather significant.

Notably, while trying to figure out how to settle into his spot alongside Curry and the rest, Durant shot a career-best 53.7 percent from the field in the regular season; in these playoffs, he is shooting 55.6 percent, while averaging 25.4 points and also playing the best defense of his career.

If you need evidence of Durant's defensive mindset, just watch the video of his chase-down block of Dejounte Murray on Monday — when Durant wanted to knock that ball out of the air so badly that he actually blocked it twice.

So yes, in that locker room and on the floor, Durant is, as Curry told me back in January, "one of us."

"You saw his game the last two games," Warriors owner Joe Lacob said of Durant. "He's been amazing. He fits perfectly. That's my greatest happiness is that he gets to go to the Finals now, he loves his teammates and fits so well in the organization. It feels so great that it worked out so well to this point."

Joe, when you were in The Hamptons for that Durant meeting, was this moment what you discussed?

"Well, not this moment — another moment beyond this moment," Lacob said with a laugh.

That's where the Warriors are right now, at the moment before the biggest moment, and they're ready for anything now. ■

Kevin Durant accepts congratulations from fans at Oracle Arena following the Warriors' Game 2 victory over the Cavaliers in the NBA Finals. (Nhat V. Meyer/Staff)

# 30
## POINT GUARD

# STEPHEN CURRY

## Curry's Leadership Style Warriors' Secret Sauce

### By Marcus Thompson II • May 29, 2017

Stephen Curry's lowest point came the night of Game 7.

The anger kidnapped his words on the silent drive home. He was girded by the presence of friends and family at his post-game gathering, but inside he was feeling it.

The frustration and disappointment. The looping mental replay of Kyrie Irving's step-back 3, of the Cavaliers celebrating on the Oracle floor. The churning in his core.

He sought comfort in the garlic crust of Domino's pizza. A glass of wine. A Cuban cigar. But all he found was dejection.

"Saddest cigar I've ever smoked," Curry said. "Usually you smoke a cigar when you win. That's how terrible of a party it was. … We had some real conversations that night about how much it sucked."

And then the low point was done, passed over him like a storm. The angst wasn't gone but the worst was over. Life had resumed. Curry's secret talent had kicked in.

He is nearly as adept at discernment as he is at shooting. Curry tends to always see the big picture, to remember the essences — of life, of basketball, of who he is and wants to be — even in the midst of adversity. He clings to perspective. And this season, after the humiliation of squandering of championship, after the Warriors became a freak show, perspective was the pipe he held onto so the storm didn't pull him away.

It's this part of Curry that goes overlooked, outshined by crossovers and transition 3-pointers. It is how he bounced back from debilitating defeat. It is why Kevin Durant is here. It is how the Warriors grew in chemistry despite all the elements endangering their bond. It is how they enter these Finals focused and driven, not fueled by revenge but by the pursuit of excellence

No, it wasn't all Curry. But it's been a key ingredient all along. It violates the superstar order but is paramount in the development and sustainability of this Warriors' era. If the Larry O'Brien trophy does return to the Bay, it will be validation for the secret ingredient in the Warriors' sauce: Curry's leadership style.

Getting their heart ripped out on the national stage, and subsequently ridiculed, didn't derail the Warriors. Adding an MVP, and with him relentless scrutiny and criticism, never seemed to penetrate this team's psyche.

And now that they are back here, in the Finals against the same Cavaliers that devastated them, revenge — a dangerous fuel for a team because of its volatility — doesn't seem to be the dominant motivator. Instead, it's basketball excellence, it's buffering each other from the rampant venom aimed their way.

And when you break down the biology of the Warriors, the origin of these intangibles is Curry. They trickle down from his seat atop the Warriors' podium and infiltrate the chemistry.

Draymond Green is the heartbeat of the team. But

After suffering disappointment in the 2016 Finals, Steph Curry led a focused, stacked Warriors team back to the biggest stage. (Jose Carlos Fajardo/Staff)

Curry is its nervous system — how the team is wired, responsible for processing the environment and situation and informing the entire organism how to respond.

"Your consistency on a daily basis, how you handle yourself, how you deal with your successes and failures," Curry said. "It's more like an 'actions speak louder' kind of situation for me. That's how I approach the leadership stand point. Humility, knowing that I have flaws, things that I gotta work on on a daily basis. … People know when I say something, it's coming from a place of honesty and care. It's not any self-serving purpose to it. That is how I approach it every day."

Curry had an out. He could have potentially killed the Durant-to-Warriors move.

He had gotten word through a friend he trusts that Durant had concerns about how Curry would receive him. This was a revelation to Curry, who had no idea he was the last hurdle in the blockbuster, maybe the decider.

What happens if he goes Kobe Bryant, who recruited Dwight Howard by making it clear whose franchise it is? Most pundits and experts would have probably praised him for marking his territory.

What if Curry does the passive aggressive thing and goes radio silent, leaving Durant with the unaddressed concern, hoping the uncertainty prevents Durant from coming?

Instead, Curry did the unthinkable. He went out of his way to make sure Durant felt welcomed, comfortable.

"I'm still not convinced …," Curry said before pausing with squinted stare as he wrestled with how to verbalize his point. "Being the man, the star, the clear-cut one, stuff like that — it's overrated if you're not winning.

"Last summer we had a decision. But in that moment, in the summer of 2016, we had the opportunity to go that way or this way. I felt like this way was the best opportunity for us as a team to win. I can live with that all day long. Yeah, I don't get to shoot 25 shots a game. I don't get to run 800 pick-and-rolls a game. Yeah, that's a sacrifice, if you want to call it that. The point is to win a bunch of championships and whatever the narrative is it doesn't really matter."

But no good deed goes unpunished. So Curry's

display of humility didn't end with his sales pitch. It ignited a process that would require persistence, more sacrifice and patience.

Curry has always set that tone in the locker room. For example, it's been years since money was a divisive issue in the Warriors' franchise. That's because it's hard to complain about money when the best player is severely underpaid yet dancing around with joy. Every other star on the roster followed by taking less money than he could have gotten. The path has been paved for Durant to do the same in July.

But past good works wouldn't cut it this season. The pressure, and attention, and stakes were such that any discord had the potential to be detrimental, especially coming from the top. Curry's example, the tone he set, was as paramount as ever.

And though the ridicule from blowing a 3-1 lead never let up, though he had fallen a tier in public perception, though his Under Armour shoes declined in sales, though he struggled initially adjusting to Durant's large presence, Curry's discernment carried the day.

Most of today's superstars have a reputation for, one way or another, flexing their superstarness. It's an accepted part of being so good, a perk that comes with the production. Yet Curry shuns the option in favor of the meek route. Discernment won't let him act on the moment at the expense of the big picture.

So his teammates can yell at him on the court publicly and there won't be a sniff of anger after the game. He can listen to analysts demean his status, fans mock his failures, and repeatedly opt not to defend his own honor.

The talk of him having a down year quietly burns him. The narrative that he hasn't played well in the NBA Finals agitates him. He would love to point out he averaged 26 in 2015, outplayed LeBron James in an epic Game 5 before controlling the closeout in Game 6. All against all-out double teams and traps.

"Only thing is if you look at it compared to what LeBron has done the last two (Finals)," Curry said, explaining the only context possible to support this idea he doesn't play well in the Finals. "He's been unbelievable. He's played amazing. Kyrie had an amazing

Stephen Curry signs autographs for fans before a game against the New Orleans Pelicans at Oracle Arena. (Jane Tyska/Staff)

series last year, an amazing three games and that won them a championship. It just depends on what you decide to focus on. But the same way I get the benefit of the doubt in some situations, I get harped on worse in other situations."

So why bother with challenging narratives? What's the win in that? What's the message that delivers to his team?

So Curry eats it, swallows his considerable pride and leans on the perspective that reminds him he is winning anyway.

"If there is a debate about my value in this league, on my team, then that's an issue to begin with," Curry said. "When you talk about a certain amount of guys in the league every year, I'm going to be one of them. And at the end of the day, we're four wins away from being

talked about a lot. So I have a job to do in that respect so who cares about all that other stuff. I'm not going to fight that battle. It's not a battle worth fighting."

The NBA has become like the Game of Thrones series. Star players are overseeing kingdoms with legions of fans, warring with one another for crowns and endorsements and the adoration that comes with both. Alliances are being forged, enemies declared, tactics and strategies being employed.

Meanwhile, Curry has built quite the kingdom. It was formed by humility and sacrifice, and is being sustained by avoiding the bait that makes empires fall.

With Curry, it's all about the long game. And being back in the Finals, with a window to be in many more, is proof his method works, too. ■

# LACOB-GREEN MUTUAL ADMIRATION SOCIETY

## Owner and Power Forward Are Two of a Kind

### By Tim Kawakami • June 1, 2017

Joe Lacob and Draymond Green are clear about this, even clearer than they usually are, and these are two guys who find it practically impossible to hide their truest, rawest emotions anyway.

Lacob, the owner of the Warriors, and Draymond Green, the team's starting power forward and centrifugal emotional force, might be the two most similarly wired members of this franchise, and together they're the team's thrumming competitive engine.

They know this. They understand it about each other and themselves. And it's a large part of who the Warriors have been, are and will continue to be, as they get set for Game 1 of the NBA Finals.

On this multilayered team, general manager Bob Myers and coach Steve Kerr are the thoughtful, mindful architects; Stephen Curry and Andre Iguodala are the calm locker-room authorities and counselors; Kevin Durant is the new and vital ingredient.

And Green and Lacob are the Warriors' heart-on-sleeve litigators, instigators and full-throttle fire-starters.

Which is why, now, a year after Green's series-turning suspension in Game 5 of the Finals against Cleveland, Lacob doesn't hesitate to maintain his 100-percent support of Green's actions back then.

"It never even crossed my mind to be mad at him," Lacob said recently of the backhand slap at LeBron James that resulted in Green's suspension. "He's a tremendous competitor. I just love the guy. He's just a fantastic competitor, plays so hard, just a great, smart player, and I support him."

The Warriors were up 3-1 in the series when Green was suspended. They lost Game 5 at Oracle Arena — Green watched from a suite at the Coliseum next door, joined by Myers — and then lost Games 6 and 7 with Green back in action.

As a tribute to Green, Lacob famously wore Green's jersey while sitting courtside during Game 5.

"I didn't really think about it at the time, just was obvious I should do that," Lacob said.

Green and Lacob were close before that game, often texting each other motivational messages and sharing the bond of two people whose lives started out far from where they are now.

But that game, and the rumbling aftermath, absolutely tied Green and Lacob, and also Green and Myers, in a profound way.

You want to know why Warriors management supports Green through the occasional bump and controversy? Because they know he fights for them on the court, with everything he has, and because Lacob and Myers understand and depend on that.

"To get suspended from Game 5 and Joe wears my jersey? How many owners are doing that?" Green said. "That goes a long way.

"To be suspended, go next door, (Myers) comes, sits with me the entire game? That stuff goes a long way.

Draymond Green and Warriors owner Joe Lacob pose with the 2015 NBA championship trophy after the Warriors defeated the Cavaliers in six games. (Nhat V. Meyer/Staff)

"But our relationship has definitely evolved over the years. No. 1, you figure out how similar personalities you have and you identify more and more with each other."

Lacob is still bothered by the circumstances and timing of Green's suspension and — very Draymond-like — isn't bashful about saying so.

Most especially Lacob points out that Green was not called for a foul when he tapped James' groin late in Game 4, but was retroactively given a Flagrant 1 by NBA discipline czar Kiki Vandeweghe. Because Green already had accumulated three Flagrant Foul points in the playoffs, this one put him over the limit.

"I certainly was not happy about him being assessed a flagrant foul by the league after the fact, a day after he was not even assessed a common foul by the referees on the floor," Lacob said.

"I have a problem with that. And the league knows that. And I did and I still do. I don't agree with that particular rule or ability for the league to do that."

Ten days ago, in the moments after clinching the Western Conference finals over San Antonio, Lacob said he thought the Warriors were the better team in last year's Finals. Does Lacob think the Warriors lost the series because of the suspension?

"Well, I'd rather not go there," Lacob said. "Certainly it contributed, it enabled to happen what did happen. But the Cavaliers certainly deserved to win the series.

"I never meant to imply otherwise. They came back from 3-1, all credit to them and they are the champions."

But Lacob, at the same time, also expressed a preference for the Cavs to emerge from the Eastern Conference finals against Boston.

"What I said ... I didn't really care who we played, truthfully just wanted to get there, for the opportunity to win a championship," said Lacob, noting he previously was a minority owner of the Celtics and would have had interest in playing Boston in these Finals, too.

"And I really don't want to speak for our players or anybody else, or coaches, just me personally, I guess I slightly would've preferred playing the Cavaliers only because I feel we lost to them last year and I personally feel like it'd be nice to have the opportunity to get it back from them."

Lacob's son, Kirk, a Warriors assistant GM, jokingly calls his father "the Draymond" of team management, and Joe Lacob considers that a large compliment.

Competitive. Edgy. Demanding. Occasionally misunderstood. Maybe sometimes a little annoying.

Yeah, Draymond gets all of that.

"My relationship with Joe is great," Green said. "You know, obviously it's evolved over the years. I think we've got that same kind of fire, same type of passion.

"Bob's the same way — Bob just is not as outspoken as Joe and I, but he's the same way. Just that same type of burning desire to be the best, to win every game, to be right on every single play."

Green is the kid from Saginaw, Michigan, who worked his way to becoming a star at Michigan State. Then Green's raw athletic skills didn't measure with many in his draft class, so he slipped to the 35th overall pick of the 2012 draft. The Warriors are very thankful for that.

Lacob was a middle-class kid who built his fortune by taking some great risks in the venture capital world. He bought the Warriors by outbidding no less than Larry Ellison, and declared immediately that the Warriors would win titles, when they were, at the time, one of the worst franchises in sports.

"In my case, I'm not the most athletic player, I don't have the greatest jump shot," Green said. "I don't have the greatest ballhandling. Like I don't have Steph's jump shot or KD's length and athleticism and ability to score or Steph and Kyrie (Irving)'s handle or Steph and Klay (Thompson)'s jump shot.

"I don't have those things. But a part of what's made me good is my desire, just my burning desire to win and to be great.

"And when you look at Joe, moreso than his smarts, what has gotten him over the edge is his burning desire to be great.

"There's a lot of smart people. He's smart. But that's not what got him over the top — it's being smart plus having the desire that not many other people have."

Green sees that in Lacob, Lacob sees that in Green, and if you're looking for either man to critique the other for a rabid competitive streak, you will be waiting a long, long time. ■

Joe Lacob gives the Warriors encouragement during a regular season game against the 76ers at Oracle Arena. (Dan Honda/Staff)

**WESTERN CONFERENCE QUARTERFINALS • GAME 1**

APRIL 16, 2017 • OAKLAND, CALIFORNIA

WARRIORS 121, TRAIL BLAZERS 109

# BLOCK PARTY

## Warriors Pull Away, Paced by Green-Led Defensive Unit

### By Anthony Slater

Danger time for the Warriors in these playoffs could come at the start of the second and fourth quarters, when coach Steve Kerr typically sends Steph Curry and Kevin Durant to the bench together.

But in the postseason opener — an entertaining 121-109 Game 1 win over the Blazers in Oracle — the Warriors used it as separation time, led by Draymond Green and a pack of veteran, motivated defenders that turned an 88-88 tie into a runaway fourth-quarter win.

CJ McCollum and Damian Lillard roasted the Warriors defense for the game's first 36 minutes, combining for 62 points in three quarters and needing only minor contributions from Portland's others to remain competitive longer than expected.

"The offense was there — we had 88 points at the end of the third quarter," Green said. "But the problem was they had 88 points. So we knew we had to get stops."

Which happens to be the speciality of this current version of the Warriors' second unit, concocted at midseason. After testing Durant out with the group in November, Kerr flipped Green into it, joining Klay Thompson, Andre Iguodala, David West and, on this day, Ian Clark.

"Coach Kerr said to me the defensive intensity of this lineup could change the game for us," Green said, recalling a December conversation.

In its trial period — and still at times — it's had extended scoring struggles. A team so used to having two of the greatest scorers in NBA history suddenly is without

either. But in Green, West, Iguodala and Thompson, they combine four of the league's smartest, sturdiest, focused defenders. In that fourth quarter moment on Sunday afternoon, that's just what the Warriors needed.

The quarter started with a Green 3 that put them up three. Then Thompson — who had a rough, disengaged Game 1 on both ends the first three quarters — draped McCollum as he came off a screen and, combined with a pressuring West, forced a turnover, the first of six fourth quarter Blazers giveaways.

"David was huge. He was huge on those ball screens," Green said of West. "Damian couldn't get downhill anymore. CJ couldn't get downhill anymore. Then we were able to get a grip (on the game)."

Portland's offense, so potent earlier, was throttled by the cranked-up pressure. Allen Crabbe followed the McCollum turnover with a missed 3. Then Al-Farouq Aminu missed from the corner. Then Crabbe bricked a contested mid-ranger. The Blazers went empty the first two minutes of the quarter as the Warrior offense crawled up four.

And that's where Ian Clark worked into it. Easily the worst defender of the group, Clark's a microwave scorer when hot. Clark has killed the Blazers all season — now 23-of-30 shooting overall in five games — so instead of going with the defensive-minded Patrick McCaw, Kerr dialed up Clark, and he delivered. In the first half, Clark had a 3, steal and lefty floater sequence. In that separation point in the fourth, he followed a layup with a corner 3 to bump the Warriors up seven at the 8:59

Klay Thompson fights for a rebound against the Portland Trail Blazers in the fourth quarter of Game 1. (Nhat V. Meyer/Staff)

mark, five of his 12 points in 11 minutes.

The defensive play that set up Clark's 3 was perfect. Thompson started it off by hounding McCollum off the ball, not allowing the Blazers to get it to him for 14 seconds. It blew up Portland's design and forced a desperate hand-off feed from Noah Vonleh 30 feet from the hoop with 10 seconds on the shot clock.

As McCollum turned the corner, he was met by a doubling West, who cut off the drive as Thompson recovered, jumped and turned a McCollum jumper into an emergency pass to the limited Aminu, who was forced to try a dribble-move against the likely Defensive Player of the Year. Aminu angled left at Green, who muscled Aminu away and forced a no-chance runner that airballed into the hands of Iguodala.

Iguodala immediately pushed the rebound upcourt and found Clark in the corner, who canned the 3 as the Oracle crowd roared. The Blazers called timeout to stem momentum. But it didn't.

Out of the break, Green swatted away a McCollum layup — the third of his five blocks — which turned into a Thompson jumper. The next possession, Lillard drove into a crowd and Green ripped away his third steal, leading to two Clark free throws. The Warriors led by 11. Then on the next possession, to cap the defensive dominance, Iguodala, West and Thompson jumped Portland's pick-and-roll attempts, forcing a late-clock Lillard layup attempt that was blocked by Green, ending in an always demoralizing shot clock violation turnover.

In all, that group served up a 15-5 run in the first six minutes of the fourth quarter, delivering Durant and Curry a double-digit cushion upon return. The two stars closed strong. Curry finished with 29 points and Durant nailed a pair of jumpers to close out an efficient 32-point night on 12-of-20 shooting.

But this game's deciding stretch was without them.

"If you have six turnovers and shoot 30 percent in the (fourth) quarter, it's going to be rough," Blazers coach Terry Stotts said. "It's a credit to their defense and we've got to be able to handle that a little bit better." ■

WESTERN CONFERENCE QUARTERFINALS • GAME 2

APRIL 19, 2017 • OAKLAND, CALIFORNIA

WARRIORS 110, TRAIL BLAZERS 81

# IN COMMAND

## Warriors Step Up the Defense to Turn Back Trail Blazers

### By Anthony Slater

Steph Curry didn't shoot well. Kevin Durant didn't shoot at all. Klay Thompson didn't pick up the offensive slack.

But the Warriors didn't need their injured all-world forward — Durant missed Game 2 with a minor calf strain — or the defining skill of their All-Star backcourt to take a commanding 2-0 lead over the Blazers in Round 1.

Instead, in their 110-81 win, the Warriors won with sturdy defense and shocking production from the center position.

Golden State's historic collection of scorers is what makes the team so marketable. But defense has been at the root of its rise from irrelevancy to perennial contention in the past half-decade. It's been a top-five defense, efficiency-wise, for four straight years. It was second this season, giving up a reasonable 101.1 points per 100 possessions as offensive numbers across the league exploded.

In Game 1, Portland's stellar backcourt erupted for 68 points in three quarters to keep the Blazers in it, until the Warriors ramped up the energy, blitzed pick-and-rolls harder and the Blazers fell off in a 7-of-26 fourth quarter to lose by 12.

In Game 2, even without Durant (a versatile shot-blocker) and Shaun Livingston (a lengthy, smart backup point guard who has a hand contusion), the shorthanded Warriors started their defensive dominance early.

Thompson, in particular, was more effective guarding CJ McCollum in the opening minutes. McCollum had 27 first-half points in Game 1, weaving to any spot he wanted and finishing with flair. In Game 2, Thompson was a bit more physical from the tip, getting into McCollum and taking away his creative space.

McCollum missed his first five shots and the Blazers made only six of their 22 attempts in the first quarter, turning it over eight times as the Warriors spiked to a 33-17 lead.

"They got away with a lot," Damian Lillard said. "They were able to play really physical and it went into their favor."

At halftime, TNT analyst Charles Barkley — commonly a Warriors pessimist — predicted a second-half shootout because "neither of these teams are good defensively." It seemed like a strange comment, given Golden State's defensive performance that preceded it. When Barkley said it, the Blazers were 18-of-51 shooting with 10 turnovers and only 46 points on 53 possessions (a frigid 86.8 offensive rating), trailing by nine at halftime.

After the Barkley comment, the Warriors only performed better defensively. In the third quarter, the Blazers went 6-of-23 shooting, turned it over seven more times and only scored 12 points, as the Warriors scored 28 and jumped up 83-58.

And this wasn't just Draymond Green exerting individual dominance, similar to Game 1. It was a team-wide effort, starting with the bigs blitzing pick-and-rolls, shutting off the air space for Lillard and McCollum, who finished a combined 9-of-34 shooting for only 23 points after dropping 75 points on 28-of-54 combined in Game 1.

"It felt like we were both surrounded by two and three

Draymond Green ends up on the floor after he was fouled on his drive to the hoop in Game 2. Green had 12 rebounds and 10 assists in the commanding win. (Ray Chavez/Staff)

guys each time we got past our defender," Lillard said.

As the Warriors bigs helped on the perimeter, the Warrior guards helped at the rim. Patrick McCaw, in a spot start for Durant, slid with Lillard and spiked his layup out of bounds on one particularly impressive third-quarter play. Then a couple minutes later, Thompson — who played a terrific defensive game — slid over from the weak-side for the ultra-rare leap and block at the rim, meeting a Lillard dunk attempt with his palm and then a staredown after the swat.

"That was impressive," Warriors coach Steve Kerr said. "I don't think I've seen that (from Thompson). That was an incredible play."

"I've had hops for awhile," Thompson said.

Through three quarters, the Blazers were 24-of-73 shooting with 17 turnovers and a microscopic 73.4 offensive rating. The Warriors led by 25 and the game was over.

As for the offense, the center spot handled that.

Curry went 6 of 18 for 19 points. Thompson went 6 of 17 for 16 points. Green had 12 rebounds and 10 assists, but missed a triple-double because he only had six points.

But Zaza Pachulia opened the scoring for the second straight game with a layup, then hit a jumper and finished 5 of 8 in his 14 solid, productive minutes. JaVale McGee one-upped him, sprinting off the bench for 15 points on 7-of-7 shooting in 13 high-energy, lob-happy minutes. Combined with David West's 3 of 5, the Warriors centers — all on tiny, below-market contracts — finished with 33 points on 15-of-20 shooting.

And on this night — when the Blazers only finished with 81 points on 33 percent shooting — that was more than enough for a dominant Game 2 win.

"People want to talk about the shooting in the backcourt and all that stuff, but this has been a great defensive team for awhile," Kerr said. "Since before I got here they were a great defensive team, which has really been the hallmark of this club for the last five years." ■

APRIL 22, 2017 • PORTLAND, OREGON

WARRIORS 119, TRAIL BLAZERS 113

# SCINTILLATING SURGE

## Without Kerr and Other Key Pieces, Warriors Rally Behind McGee, Thompson

### By Anthony Slater

The Warriors didn't have their star small forward, their head coach and two key bench pieces. But Game 3 showcased the benefit of all the gluttony they've built.

Three All-Stars, a seasoned assistant coach, a former Finals MVP and a revived 7-foot pogo-stick center remained, all combining for a thrilling 119-113 comeback win in Portland, giving the Warriors a commanding 3-0 series lead and allowing their ailing co-workers needed rest without repercussions.

Kevin Durant remained sidelined because of his ailing calf. An ill Steve Kerr remained in his hotel room for the game. Shaun Livingston and Matt Barnes remained out.

The Blazers took advantage of those absences early. They blasted out to an 11-3 lead in the opening minutes and maintained a hefty cushion for most of the first 30 minutes.

Damian Lillard and CJ McCollum — held completely in check by the Warriors in Game 2 (23 combined points on 9-of-34 shooting) — returned home and returned to form in Game 3. The duo finished with 63 combined on 20 of 46, with most of that damage done in the first three quarters. When McCollum nailed a transition 3, set up by Lillard, with 8:30 left in the third quarter to put the Blazers up 16, the smell of blowout filled the Moda Center.

The Warriors, lazy and late to get back in transition on the play, looked ready to concede Game 3 and round up the sidelined cavalry for a huge Game 4.

But midway through the third quarter, JaVale McGee entered the game and the team's energy level bolted. McGee — a camp invite snatched off the scrap heap and not guaranteed a roster spot — has continually produced when called upon in small spurts this season. He was huge in Games 1 and 2. He was even bigger in Game 3.

Using his size advantage, McGee made himself available a few times high in the air, finishing an outrageous reach-back lob dunk, set up by Draymond Green, and another less outrageous but equally important layup lob, again set up by Green, to key the game-changing run.

The Warriors were electrified by McGee and the previously cold Klay Thompson turned into a microwave. He only scored seven first half points and missed both of his 3s. But right out of halftime, acting head coach Mike Brown drew up a beautiful play design that freed up Thompson for a wide open wing look. He buried it and his fuse was lit.

"(Mike Brown) was the MVP tonight," Green said.

Thompson made his first four 3s in the third quarter, including a personal 8-0 run, when he sandwiched two free throws with two big 3s. The second of which was set up by a ferocious McGee and Stephen Curry trap at halfcourt, forcing McCollum into a rushed

Portland's Damian Lillard tries to get a shot off against Klay Thompson (11), Ian Clark (21) and James Michael McAdoo (20). Lillard scored 31 points in the loss but needed 23 shots to do so. (Nhat V. Meyer/Staff)

pass, which was stolen by Thompson. The 3 brought the Warriors within four.

Another Thompson 3 a few minutes later was followed by a runout fastbreak ending in a tomahawk Andre Iguodala dunk, which tied the game at 83. When McGee made a layup on the following possession, the Warriors had their largest lead of the game to that point: 85-83, late in the third quarter.

McGee finished with 14 points on 6-of-8 shooting in 16 minutes. He is 15-of-20 shooting for 35 points in 37 minutes during this series.

"You guys saw: He was fantastic," Brown said of McGee.

But a back-and-forth fourth quarter remained. With 5:35 left, an Evan Turner jumper trimmed the Warriors lead to 100-98. Curry, after a quiet start, did the honor of putting Portland away. A series of Iguodala dunks —

four in the second half — had the Warriors up 104-100 with 61 seconds left. But Iguodala missed an open 3 and the Blazers, with a rebound, could tighten it up.

But they couldn't get the rebound. Rookie Patrick McCaw — who replaced Durant with an impressive 11-point, five rebound, five-assist, three-steal night — slid in to steal away the rebound and pitch it out to an open Curry at the top of the key.

Curry stepped into and planted the dagger 3 to put the Warriors up seven with 49 seconds left. The Blazers tried to crawl back in the closing seconds, but Curry followed up the 3 with a fadeaway and four free throws, giving him nine of his game-high 35 points in the final minute and delivering the Warriors an incredible comeback victory and 3-0 series lead.

"A heck of a win by our guys," Brown said. ■

# TEAM TAKEDOWN

## Curry's 37 Leads Warriors as Blowout Wraps Up Sweep

### By Anthony Slater

To get this lopsided first-round series done as quickly as possible, the Warriors got Monday night's clinching Game 4 done as quickly as possible — as in, Portland looked like toast midway through the first quarter.

The Warriors scored the night's first 14 points, led 28-5 six minutes into it, planted 45 first-quarter points on the overmatched, ready-to-vacation Blazers and ran away with a dominating 128-103 win to complete an easy four-game sweep.

"Indescribable," Blazers coach Terry Stotts said.

"Unbelievable," said Mike Brown, handling the head-coaching duties for ailing Steve Kerr for the second straight game.

The news pregame was of the return of Kevin Durant, who was held out of the two previous games with a minor calf strain because the Warriors could prioritize rest without much fear of repercussions in the loss column.

Without Durant — but still with three other All-Stars and a capable supporting cast — the Warriors looked great and won both games. With Durant in Game 4, they looked even greater.

Durant hit the game's first shot, a confident pull-up 3 from the right wing just feet from his mother, Wanda, seated courtside. Durant uncoiled that 7-foot frame and released it from an unblockable height. When it splashed through, Wanda turned around, drink in hand, and clinked her glass with Rich Kleiman, Durant's business partner, sitting a row behind her.

The moment and ensuing minutes were the latest reminder of the league's worst nightmare, concocted this past July Fourth weekend in the Hamptons. Durant followed up the 3 with a cutting transition dunk, set up smoothly by Stephen Curry. Then he erased a Maurice Harkless fastbreak dunk attempt with a burst of acceleration, a leap and an impressive LeBron-like chasedown block.

A few minutes later, when his crossover and soaring dunk put the Warriors up 22-3, worries that Durant's twinged calf muscle would slow him were out the window. From there, he floated to the background and didn't do much else, finishing with 10 points and only seven shots in 20 easy minutes — almost like he came out and used the Blazers as a scout team test run for his calf, proved to himself it was fine and then let the other stars stick Portland with the final daggers.

"That was the plan," Durant said.

Curry was first in line. The Warriors' star point guard played his most dominant game of the series. Curry nailed three of the team's eight first-quarter 3s, closed the first half with a fadeaway 26-footer as he fell to the floor and shimmied as Golden State's lead ballooned to 72-48.

Draymond Green and Steph Curry celebrate a basket in Game 4 of Golden State's sweep over Portland. Curry had 37 points and Green had 21 points in the dominant win. (Ray Chavez/Staff)

Curry then closed his night with another deep third-quarter barrage, highlighted by a straightaway 3 in which he turned, nonchalantly, right as he released it, high-fiving Draymond Green and not even looking as the ball splashed through.

"That was the shot that felt the best in a long, long time," Curry said. "But I've actually missed some where I've done that before, so I'm not flawless with it."

In all, Curry made seven of his 11 shots from beyond the arc and finished with 37 points on 12-of-20 shooting — plus eight assists and seven rebounds — in 29 minutes. He didn't even play a second of the fourth quarter.

But it wasn't just the megastars. It was everyone. As was the case this entire series, the Warriors didn't get a poor performance from anywhere in their rotation. Even the maligned Zaza Pachulia scored a series-high 11 points on 4-of-5 shooting, including an and-1 in that runaway first quarter in which he celebrated with a snow angel on the court after tumbling. All five Warriors starters scored in double-figures, while three Blazers starters (CJ McCollum, Meyers Leonard and Harkless) combined for eight points total.

Green blocked three more Blazers shots in Game 4, giving him a playoff-high 17 blocks in four games. But he provided much more than defense. Green's 3-point shot was on the entire series. He made five of his eight 3s in Game 4 and finished the series 11-of-20 from deep.

Klay Thompson chipped in 18 points and JaVale McGee capped his breakout series with the highlight of the night. McGee cocked back and rammed through an outrageous (and overthrown) alley-oop feed, plus the foul, which sent the Warriors bench into a frenzy. It came with 1:54 left in the first quarter. It put the Warriors up 43-16. It was the unofficial punctuation on an easy series, resulting in at least five days of rest for a nicked up team.

"I've been in this situation before as a head coach and certain teams and certain guys, you worry about having this much time off," Brown said. "But I truly believe (the rest) is good for this group." ■

JaVale McGee rejects the Portland Trail Blazers' Shabazz Napier at the rim, one of three blocks for McGee in the win. (Ray Chavez/Staff)

# DRAYMOND'S KIND OF GAME

## Golden State Uses Rest, Defense to Cruise to 1-0 Series Lead

### By Anthony Slater

Draymond Green and Steph Curry miscommunicated on a second quarter inbound that wasn't even being defended, leading to an overthrow and the type of careless turnover that, if capitalized upon, can breathe life into the underdog but resourceful Jazz.

But Utah didn't capitalize. Draymond Green destroyed a should-be 2-on-1 score — unofficially the 987th fastbreak he's busted up this season — stripping a Gordon Hayward layup, then pushing it ahead for an eventual Kevin Durant dunk, as a quartet of fans in section 101 rose with signs to spell out D(efensive) P(layer) O(f the) Y(ear).

There were stars all over the court in Game 1, but no one really starred in the Warriors' workman-like 106-94 win over the Jazz. But that's the kind of game — and this is the kind of matchup — that so perfectly fits Green.

The Warriors were idle the seven days prior, awaiting their second round opponent after sweeping through the Blazers. There was concern about some possible early rust.

And maybe there was a bit, at least offensively. Steph Curry and Kevin Durant both airballed in the first few minutes. The Warriors didn't score on the first few possessions. It took them more than five minutes to reach 10 points. But it took nearly four minutes for Utah to score at all.

That included a Jazz shot clock violation before a Jazz point. After bleeding the clock under five seconds, lanky center Rudy Gobert found himself about six feet from the hoop, needing to make a play against Zaza Pachulia. But as he gathered for a hook, Green pounced, double-teaming a stunned Gobert and causing him to fumble it away.

There was a lot of that early for the Jazz. The change of defensive speed from the Clippers to the Warriors — particularly Green's — seemed to throttle them. They missed their first five shots and turned it over three times, as Golden State crawled to a 7-0 lead.

"One of the things about Golden State is just how quick they think," Jazz coach Quin Snyder said. "Just mentally, they're able to get, not just from possession to possession, but within a possession."

The Jazz steadied a bit, adjusted and remained competitive for patches of the night. When Green left midway through the first quarter, they cut the lead to 27-21 by the start of the second.

But that's when the Warriors planted maybe their most dominant spurt of the night. Green opened the second quarter by bolting back from a defensive

Draymond Green runs into fans during the Game 1 win over Utah. Green had 17 points, eight rebounds and six assists in the game. (Nhat V. Meyer/Staff)

assignment on the perimeter for a block of a Derrick Favors layup, already Green's 18th block in five playoff games. It led to a David West layup on the other end.

Green fed West for a layup a minute later and then, the possession after, nailed a wing 3. The Blazers continually left Green open on the perimeter in Round 1 — a wise strategy considering the surrounding weapons and Green's inaccuracy this season (under 33 percent). But he punished the Blazers, making 11 of his 20 3s and he again punctured a Jazz defense that deployed a similar strategy in Game 1, making two of five.

"Early on in the season, my shot didn't feel good at all," Green said. "Just really didn't feel used to the ball. As the season's gone on, I feel like I've got my rhythm back… Riding high on the confidence (right now)."

Green is now 13-of-25 from deep in the postseason. He finished with 17 points on the night, including a rumbling transition dunk just after that first 3, sprinting the Warriors up 14 early in the second quarter. He was the engine of their sturdy defensive start and the spark for their offensive separation. Green was a plus-19 in his 34 minutes.

From there, the Warriors mostly cruised, as their lead fluctuated from just under 10 to around 20 and settled at a non-dramatic 12. No one stole the show offensively. Steph Curry had 22 points on 11 shots — his night highlighted by a ridiculous crossover of Jazz behemoth Rudy Gobert, spinning him in a circle before hitting a reverse layup.

"I had the best seat in the house," Mike Brown said. "And I didn't even pay for it."

Kevin Durant had 17. Klay Thompson had 15. Pachulia had 10. No one on the Jazz had more than 13.

"Next game we need to come out with energy," Kevin Durant said. "We can't be relaxed. Relaxed teams, happy teams get beat." ■

Steph Curry goes behind his back with Utah's George Hill attempting to keep up. Curry had 22 points in the victory. (Nhat V. Meyer/Staff)

WESTERN CONFERENCE SEMIFINALS • GAME 2
MAY 4, 2017 • OAKLAND, CALIFORNIA
WARRIORS 115, JAZZ 104

# PAIN AND GAIN

## Green Does it All, Shakes Off Fall in Gritty Triumph

### By Anthony Slater

The biggest scare in Game 2 wasn't delivered by the Jazz, who, through two games and two losses, have shown just enough grit to keep it mildly competitive but not enough firepower to legitimately concern the Warriors.

Nope, the biggest scare was delivered by Draymond Green, who, after starring for the game's first 40 minutes, took a hard fall and then a slipping tumble as he tried to get up, grabbing his left knee and staying down, as the arena went silent.

They'd rise again soon after, as Green returned from the locker room to the bench and eventually the court, helping the Warriors finish off a Game 2 win 115-104 to take a commanding 2-0 series lead to Utah. The status of that left leg will be a topic in the hours before Game 3, but for now it seems the Warriors dodged a bullet.

And it was quite the dangerous bullet, considering how well Green is currently playing.

In Round 1, Green dominated the Blazers with his defense, blocking 17 shots in four games and terrorizing every inch of the court. But lost within his defensive dominance was some surprising sharpshooting. Green made 11 of his 20 3s against Portland.

That hot streak has now leaked over into the Utah series.

Green opened Game 2 scorching hot from deep, nailing four first quarter 3s as Utah continually left Green wide open and he continually made them pay.

"Obviously their gameplan is to have whoever's guarding Draymond sit in the lane," Mike Brown said. "So he's getting wide-open threes and, knock on wood, hopefully he'll keep shooting the ball the way he's been shooting it throughout the playoffs and make them pay."

Earlier in the season, Green hit five 3s in Salt Lake City and later revealed that his aggressiveness was because he'd heard a comment from Jazz coach Quin Snyder that his team wouldn't gameplan for Green's deep shot.

The strategy seems wise. Green dipped from 38 percent down to below 31 percent from 3 this season, struggling to make open shots and — with Klay Thompson, Steph Curry and Kevin Durant roaming the court — a Green 3 seems like a win for the opponent.

"I find myself particularly open in every matchup," Green said. "That probably won't change."

But similar to Game 7 of the Finals last season — when Green hit six of eight 3s — his stroke has returned at the season's most important time.

Those four 3s blasted the Warriors out to a 33-15 first quarter lead, allowing them to bob in and out of focus the rest of the night, pawing away the gritty Jazz every time they climbed near or within single digits.

The Warriors reverted to some concerning ways at

Draymond Green fights for the ball against the Utah Jazz's Rudy Gobert in Game 2. Green had another impressive all-around game with 21 points, seven rebounds, six assists and four steals. (Nhat V. Meyer/Staff)

times in Game 2. After only turning it over seven times in Game 1, they coughed it up 17 times in Game 2 — often carelessly and in the open court, allowing Utah some easy hoops (22 points off Golden State turnovers).

But it wasn't just the turnovers that kept Utah in it. It was some occasionally lazy defense. To start the second half, the Warriors yawned as Joe Johnson planted a corner 3 and then, because of a defensive breakdown in transition, let Shelvin Mack walk into a wide open wing 3. Mike Brown called a timeout 44 seconds into the second half.

But the Warriors would respond to any mild threat, bolting back up on the strength of a sturdy game up and down their rotation. Kevin Durant was particularly effective, going for 25 points, 11 rebounds and seven important assists — including the game-sealer for an Andre Iguodala dunk. Durant made 13 of his 15 free throws.

Steph Curry had 23 points, Klay Thompson chipped in 14 and Iguodala, who is now a frigid 0-of-18 from 3 in the playoffs, contributed elsewhere, dunking three times and scoring 10 points.

But Green, again, was the star, continuing his torrid run through the postseason. He had seven rebounds, six assists and another block, his 20th in six playoff games. But his most important attribute was his rarest: the 3-point shot.

Green finished with five 3s, tying Curry for a team-high. He now has 18 in the playoffs, which is more than Klay Thompson (16), LeBron James (15) and Kevin Love (13), among some of the league's other sharpshooters.

"Hopefully that jumper travels," Curry said of Green.

Green's strong play only made that late injury scare more concerning for the Warriors. After an errant layup on a fourth quarter drive, Green tumbled down at the baseline and got a bit tangled up with Rudy Gobert. As Green tried to get up, he seemed to slip and his left leg bent strangely. Green crumbled to the floor, grabbed at his knee and stayed down for a minute, before limping to the locker room.

But after the game, he said the knee just "locked up" a bit — something he said he dealt with before. He doesn't believe it'll affect him in Game 3.

"I'll be fine," Green said. "One time I had one in college and I outrebounded Michigan two days later. Their whole team." ■

Steph Curry's family is a consistent presence at Warriors' playoff games, including his brother Seth (left), a guard for the Dallas Mavericks, and his dad Dell, a former NBA sharpshooter. (Nhat V. Meyer/Staff)

WESTERN CONFERENCE SEMIFINALS • GAME 3
MAY 6, 2017 • SALT LAKE CITY, UTAH
WARRIORS 102, JAZZ 91

# TOUGH GET GOING

## Warriors Weather First Big Challenge of Playoffs, Go Up 3-0

### By Anthony Slater

At some point, when the competition heightens in this postseason — against Houston or San Antonio or Cleveland — you expect more consistent situations like Game 3: The Warriors, with under four minutes left, protecting a two-point lead, not marinating in another double-digit blowout.

After failing to lead for even a second out in Oakland, the Jazz returned home and pushed the Warriors into a pressurized crunch-time situation — 86-84 Golden State, 3:56 left, a practice test for what's likely to come.

The Warriors passed, outscoring the Jazz by nine in the final four minutes to sprint away with a 102-91 win, jump up 3-0 in the series and put themselves one final step from a second straight sweep and another week of rest.

Cold most of the night, Steph Curry jumpstarted the closing spurt. After a drive and kickback pass to Andre Iguodala, Curry weaved around a Draymond Green down screen and, when Rodney Hood failed to recognize and help in time, Curry jetted off Green's shoulder, caught and planted a wing 3 to put the Warriors up 89-84.

"Never lose your aggressiveness," Curry said.

On the next possession, Kevin Durant — scorching hot most of the night — went a simpler route to shove his dagger. All night, the Warriors attacked Rudy Gobert in the pick-and-roll with Durant. Gobert likes to protect the rim, so he sags back on screens. That's unwise on one of these nights from Durant, where the 7-footer is rising and splashing jumper after jumper (he went 12-of-18 outside the paint).

So Durant coiled off the screen and immediately rose from the wing, as Gobert stood a few too many feet away — a 7-foot-1 but unable to even contest as Durant rainbowed through his fourth 3. It put the Warriors up 92-84 — a 6-0 run by the Warriors' two former MVPs in 34 seconds to provide the necessary separation.

"They made some unbelieveable shots that were timely," Quin Snyder said. "That's why they are who they are. They set a great screen and Steph broke open…KD is seven feet tall. He rose up and he's playing like who he is. You could search for answers and often the answer is right in front of our bench. Those are two great players."

Suddenly up eight with three minutes left, the Warriors only needed a couple backbreakers to seal it. Durant provided them.

After a strong Game 1 to open the playoffs against Portland, he has been quiet the last couple weeks, missing two games against the Blazers with a twinged calf and then slowly working his way back, slumping mostly into the offensive background, by Durant's usual standards.

Kevin Durant takes a shot over Utah's Rudy Gobert in the Game 3 victory. Durant had 38 points and 13 rebounds in the win. (Nhat V. Meyer/Staff)

Not in Game 3. With Curry struggling (despite the hot finish, he still closed 6-of-20 shooting) and Klay Thompson remaining way off (1-of-9 shooting), Durant shouldered the offensive load. He was aggressive in the first quarter, taking 10 shots and scoring 13 points.

After a slow start to the second quarter with Durant on the bench, which included Utah taking its first lead of the series 10 quarters into it, Durant returned and the Warriors went OKC-like iso ball with him in the mid-post.

Three times, they delivered it to him 15 feet from the hoop and then cleared out. Three straight times, he outmuscled the smaller Gordon Hayward to his spot and then drilled an unblockable fadeaway over Hawyard's outstretched arms. At one point, Durant had 27 points and no other Warrior had more than seven.

In the closing minutes, Durant was more fired up than usual. After chirping at a courtside fan, who among other things was screaming about Durant's "legacy," Durant zipped to one of his favorite spots — 15 feet out, near the elbow — and sunk another 15-footer, putting the Warriors up 11 with 2:09 left. After the jumper, he turned and hooted at the courtside fan, who shrugged in frustration.

Thirty seconds later, Gobert delivered a hard shove to Durant as he was posting up. Infuriated — as Durant was a couple minutes earlier when he yelled at the Jazz mascot to "get off the court" toward the end of a timeout — Durant sprinted at Gobert, shoved him and then yelled at him. After review, Durant was called for a flagrant foul and a technical.

"Just basketball," Durant said. "That's why they call our league soft. Because we call flagrants for stuff like that."

In the aftermath, acting coach Mike Brown sprinted on the court to separate Durant and told him: "Hey, we got one more game."

But 90 seconds still remained in Game 3. And to seal it, Durant delivered one final backbreaker, tossing in a banked 22-footer to give him 38 points on 15-of-26 shooting.

This season, the Warriors struggled at times down the stretch of close games. That included the Durant trip in Cleveland on Christmas and the memorable Durant isolation mishap during a late, emotional collapse against the Grizzlies.

Because of regular blowouts, there hasn't been a ton of time since for Durant and the Warriors to shore up late-game concerns. In Game 3, the Jazz provided it and Durant and the Warriors took it, icing the game with a 16-7 run that puts them on the brink of the Western Conference finals. ∎

Golden State big man David West battles Rudy Gobert for the rebound. The Warriors had a 57-51 edge on the glass in the win. (Nhat V. Meyer/Staff)

# SWEPT AWAY

## Golden State Completes Series Win Over Utah, Advances to Conference Finals

### By Anthony Slater

Just like they did to the Blazers two weeks earlier, the Warriors punched the Jazz in the mouth to start Game 4, putting what seemed to be an early cap on their closing statement.

But unlike the Blazers, the tougher Jazz clawed back and forced the Warriors to at least work into the fourth quarter, before Golden State eventually exterminated Utah's season: a 121-95 final, another Warriors' 4-0 sweep and an advancement to their third straight Western Conference Finals.

A rested, steamrolling Warriors team will be awaiting their opponent as monster favorites, having won 23 of their last 24 games dating back to mid-March and all eight of their playoff games by margins of 12, 29, 6, 25, 12, 11, 11 and 26 points.

But there were at least tiny moments of adversity in Game 4.

Early on, it didn't look like it'd be that way. After hitting only one shot in a slow Game 3, Klay Thompson opened the scoring with a pair of jumpers. Then Steph Curry hit a pair of 3s. Then Kevin Durant found Curry on a creative give-and-go layup on a baseline out of bounds play.

Meanwhile, the Jazz offense slumped against a locked in Warriors defense, missing their first 10 two-point shots and going only 6-of-25 in the first quarter. A 12-3 lead became a 21-7 lead became a 39-17 first quarter cushion — similar to the 45-22 first quarter they popped on the Blazers in Game 4.

"We talked about getting off to a good start," Mike Brown said. "Our guys did that. But maybe I should've said let's get off to a good start and keep playing that way. That's the part I may have left out."

Utah responded with a 14-2 flurry to start the second quarter, slicing through a now too relaxed Warriors defense as a surprisingly sluggish David West failed to protect the rim. Derrick Favors rammed a dunk on Draymond Green — the first time Green has rotated over, met an opponent at the rim and lost in this postseason — and then electric young point guard Dante Exum hammered one home.

The Jazz parlayed that strong second quarter start with an 8-0 close, trimming the Warriors lead from 22 all the way down to eight by halftime. Then in the third quarter, they briefly kept it close. After a defensive breakdown led to a Shelvin Mack 3, which cut it to seven, Durant and Curry chirped at each other about the breakdown. Mike Brown called timeout. On his way to the huddle, a frustrated Curry kicked a seat cushion into the stands.

Draymond Green challenges Rudy Gobert's shot in Golden State's series-clinching Game 4 win. Green tallied yet another triple-double with 17 points, 10 rebounds and 11 assists. (Nhat V. Meyer/Staff)

"I meant to," Curry said.

"Beef," Draymond Green joked.

"Chemistry issues," Durant added.

But that moment of pressure only refocused a Warriors team that proved far superior to the Jazz in the second round.

Out of the timeout, JaVale McGee hit a twisting layup and a rare jumper. Draymond Green hit his third 3 of the game and 20th in eight playoff games, turning and staring at a heckling fan in a light blue shirt behind the Warriors bench that had been heckling him.

"He told me I'd shoot us out of the series," Green said. "I don't know if he keeps stats very well, but he's not very smart. I like messing with fans. It's fun."

Golden State's defense locked back in and its offense erupted again. If there was an offensive star to be chosen — and you had your choice of many — it was Curry, who efficiently put the Jazz to sleep with 30 points on 15 shots. In his 35 minutes, the Warriors outscored the Jazz by 35 points.

Durant wasn't nearly as productive as Game 3, when he popped 38 points, but his 18 points were pretty timely. During one of Utah's second quarter runs, he stemmed the tide with a pair of jumpers. Then during a third quarter spurt, he silenced the noise again with a big wing 3 followed by a lob dunk, set up by Draymond Green.

Durant finished with 18, Green had 17, Thompson had 21 on 16 shots and McGee was the fifth Warrior in double-figures, putting up 12 points in 11 minutes off the bench without even using his trusty lob game.

And while the Jazz held sturdy at times, there really was never any doubt. Utah didn't lead for a second in Game 1, Game 2 or the closeout Game 4, only sneaking ahead for about eight minutes in Game 3, before ceding it right back to the dominant Warriors, who roll on to the Conference Finals yet to be truly tested.

"B-minus," Green said of his team's playoff performance to this point. ■

Kevin Durant soars to the rim to finish with a dunk. Durant had 18 points in the comfortable Game 4 romp. (Nhat V. Meyer/Staff)

# GREAT ESCAPE

## Warriors Rally from 25 Down to Upend Spurs in Instant Classic

### By Anthony Slater

Midway through the third quarter of Game 1, with the Spurs up by a comfortable 21 points, Kawhi Leonard took a step-back, high-rising corner fadeaway that — because he missed but was fouled — won't even register in the official stat sheet.

But the result of the play altered the game and, potentially, changed the rest of the West Finals.

Upon landing, Leonard's left foot landed on Zaza Pachulia's right, twisting Leonard's left ankle and sending him limping to the locker room for good. The Warriors immediately rattled off an 18-0 run and, over the next 20 minutes, outscored the Spurs by 25 points to rumble back for a wild 113-111 Game 1 win in Oracle.

From tip to the point of Leonard's injury, the Spurs had complete control. They jumped on a shell-shocked, out-of-rhythm Warriors team, making the easy passes difficult, turning the difficult passes into turnovers and holding one of the best offenses in league history to 16 first quarter points, while turning them over eight times and bolting up by as many as 25 in the first half.

Draymond Green made some strange, critical first half passes and mistakes. Klay Thompson was held to six points for the entire game. The Warriors were outscored by 19 in Andre Iguodala's 10 minutes before Mike Brown rested him the entire second half because "he looked hobbled" (the Warriors later called it a left knee soreness).

The Warriors trailed by 20 at halftime, when Steve Kerr gave the team an impassioned speech. Out of the break, they scored on the first four possessions. But the Spurs kept planting backbreaking jumpers. Four minutes into the third quarter, the lead had actually grown from 20 to 21.

The Kerr-driven halftime energy boost had been countered. Pau Gasol stole a Steph Curry pass with 8:17 left in the third quarter, the 12th of their 17 turnovers. Leonard maneuvered his way to the deep left corner with 7:54 left in the third, creating space for a jumper after getting Pachulia on a switch.

The play led to free throws, which put the Spurs up 23. But the foul also reinjured an ankle that had already been bothering Leonard. He originally twisted in late in Game 5 of the last series, missed the closeout Game 6 in Houston and returned for Game 1 of the West Finals looking more than fine.

Leonard had 26 points in his 23 minutes. But on a similar shot in the corner moments before the Pachulia foul, Leonard twisted his ankle on teammate David Lee, who was on the Spurs bench. He asked out of the game,

Andre Iguodala defends Spurs forward Kawhi Leonard, who would later suffer an ankle injury that helped derail San Antonio's chances of winning Game 1. (Jose Carlos Fajardo/Staff)

then returned again, only to twist it worse on Pachulia's foot, knocking him out for the rest of Game 1 and maybe beyond.

Slow-motion video of the play surfaced online soon after. Pachulia came under heat from some, with some saying it was reckless and wondering whether it was on purpose.

"That's really stupid," Pachulia said.

"Did he step under it, like on purpose?" Leonard said. "No, he was contesting the shot, the shot clock was coming down."

"I did my part to challenge the shot," Pachulia said. "It was a hand-off situation. My teammate was behind the screen. That's what I did, turned around for the rebound and that was it. I hate that anybody going down like that with injury. I'm an athlete, too. I know how it feels. Wish nothing serious for him because we are colleagues."

"You can't listen to people on Twitter," Kevin Durant said. "They're irrational."

Regardless of how it happened, it happened. And suddenly the Spurs, already without starting point guard Tony Parker for the rest of the season, were without their MVP candidate, who, to that point, was the best player on the floor.

The Warriors pounced at the opportunity. Well, primarily, Steph Curry and Kevin Durant pounced. In the ensuing 18-0 run, which lit Oracle Arena up like nothing else this season, Curry hit a huge 3 and a 22-footer with his big toe on the line. Durant had two free throws, a layup and a drive and slam on slow-footed Kyle Anderson, Leonard's replacement, who had little chance to slow Durant.

The Spurs stabilized a bit late in the third, but could only hold off the next avalanche for so long. Over the game's final 20 minutes, Durant scored 20 of his 34 points, including a weaving fourth quarter layup that gave the Warriors their first lead since early in the game, and Curry scored 15 of his game-high 40, including a floater in the final minute that served as the game-sealing hoop.

The MVP duo combined for 74 of the team's 113 points, shouldering the load for a 25-point comeback win that turned a still-impressive Spurs Game 1 performance into a gut-punch loss, leaving them down 1-0 in the series and unsure of the status of their star forward. ■

Despite being fouled by Jonathon Simmons, Kevin Durant still scores two of his 34 points in the Warriors' Game 1 victory. (Ray Chavez/Staff)

**WESTERN CONFERENCE FINALS • GAME 2**

MAY 16, 2017 • OAKLAND, CALIFORNIA

WARRIORS 136, SPURS 100

# NOT EVEN CLOSE

## Warriors Come Out Strong and Keep Going for a Decisive Game 2 Victory

### By Anthony Slater

The Warriors rarely start two straight games poorly, so you figured they'd be locked in to open Game 2. The wounded Spurs were without their star forward and starting point guard, so you figured a road clunker could be in the offing.

But Game 2 became more than a blowout. An annihilation occurred: Warriors 136, Spurs 100, a 36-point destruction that improved the Warriors to 10-0 in the playoffs and pushed them up 2-0 in the West Finals as the series shifts to San Antonio.

The Spurs never led in Game 2. The Warriors were up by as many as 41. And it was only tied for 57 seconds. On the Warriors' second possession, Kevin Durant used a hard Zaza Pachulia screen and the threat of his drive to stick a 15-footer over a late-to-react Pau Gasol.

Two trips later — after swarming Warriors defense forced the Spurs into an errant Danny Green 59-foot heave at the end of the shot clock — Draymond Green nailed an open 3 from the top of the key to make it 5-0. Green made another 3 later in the first quarter and is now 23-of-48 from deep in the playoffs, burning opponents at a scorching 48 percent clip on a shot they usually gameplan to give up.

The Warriors' third hoop: a rare Zaza Pachulia dunk. After becoming the unlikely story of the series —

after his aggressive closeout sprained the ankle of Spurs star Kawhi Leonard, turning Game 1 and forcing him to miss Game 2 — Pachulia was criticized heavily by Spurs coach Gregg Popovich during the off-day.

But the public heat didn't affect Pachulia's play. He had four rebounds and two assists in seven first quarter minutes, highlighted by that dive, catch and dunk off a nifty Steph Curry assist. But because Pachulia doesn't rise up much, the rare exertion apparently hurt the big man.

Pachulia didn't return to the game after halftime and his status for Game 3 is unknown with what the team deemed a right heel contusion. He'll get an MRI on Wednesday. He joins Andre Iguodala, who missed Game 2 with a left knee contusion, as the second Warriors' rotation player on the injury list.

But other than that, nothing else went wrong for the Warriors. That 7-2 lead was quickly 22-10 and then 33-16 by the end of the first quarter, as the wounded Spurs wilted.

"I think we maybe felt it too much, Kawhi being gone," Gregg Popovich said. "As I watched, I don't think they believed. And you have to believe. I don't think as a group they really did, which means probably a little bit feeling sorry for themselves psychologically, subconsciously, whatever psycho-babble word you want

Part of a defensive effort that held the Spurs to 37 percent shooting, Warriors defenders Klay Thompson and Matt Barnes envelop Jonathon Simmons. (Jose Carlos Fajardo/Staff)

to use. That's the way I process it. I don't think they started the game with a belief. And it showed in the lack of edge, intensity, grunts, all that sort of thing. That was disappointing."

At the root of the destruction was a locked in Warriors defense, sensing blood without San Antonio's best playmaker in the building. They shut down LaMarcus Aldridge (only eight points on 4-of-11 shooting overall) and held the Spurs to 6-of-26 shooting and four turnovers in the first quarter.

"LaMarcus has to score for us," Popovich said. "He can't be timid. He turned down shots in the first quarter. He can't do it. You've got to score. Scoring has to come from some place. I think he's got a major responsibility in Game 3 to come out and get something done."

At the same time, Steph Curry was uncorking his second straight monster game. After dropping 40 points and seven 3s in Game 1, Curry made four first quarter 3s in Game 2, scoring 15 of Golden State's first 33 points.

"It's fun to watch," Durant said. "He gets everybody else going when he gets hot like that, creates open shots for everybody else."

He took it relatively easy the rest of the night, only needing 13 shots to score 29 points in 30 minutes. He's now scored 69 points on 39 shots in this series.

Six of Curry's eight makes were 3s, giving him an NBA-high 45 threes in 10 playoff games. The next closest player: Boston's Isaiah Thomas, who has 34 made 3s in 13 playoff games.

"He's shooting two or three feet behind the 3-point line," Durant said of Curry. "It's impressive."

But Curry wasn't alone. Klay Thompson still didn't have a breakout game — scoring only 11 after mustering only six points in Game 1 — but he did plant a pair of 3s. So did Durant, who finished with 16 points after his huge 34-point Game 1, and Green, who had 13.

Three other Warriors finished in double-figures: Shaun Livingston (10), Ian Clark (10) and Patrick McCaw's, whose 18 points and 26 impactful minutes were a major bright spot in the absence of Iguodala.

All of it together produced a 36-point win, which is the second largest playoff victory in franchise history and the largest since the Philadelphia Warriors won a playoff game by 39 way back in 1948. ∎

Steph Curry, who scored 15 of Golden State's first 33 points, smiles after making a basket during the Warriors' blowout victory. (Nhat V. Meyer/Staff)

# STRANGLEHOLD

## Durant's 19-Point Third Quarter Helps Push Spurs to the Brink

### By Anthony Slater

Wounded and wobbly, the Spurs, trailing 2-0 in the series and clawing from behind in the third quarter, needed one more forceful shove to push their fading season onto life support.

Kevin Durant delivered the blow, squashing a desperate Spurs rally with a 19-point third quarter to bump the Warriors back into cruise control as they finished off a 120-108 Game 3 win in San Antonio, giving them a 3-0 stranglehold on these West Finals.

The Warriors are now 48 minutes from a third straight Finals, likely against Cleveland for a third straight time. Twelve wins gets them there. Their 11th playoff win — needing only 11 games to do so — came in Game 3, where Durant's 12 third quarter minutes catapulted them.

"He was huge for us," Mike Brown said. "We didn't do anything tricky. He got hot."

But he was quiet early on. JaVale McGee was the first Warrior in double-figures. The Warriors' backup center, only used for 15 minutes in the first two games, stepped into a starting role with Zaza Pachulia out with a heel contusion.

The Spurs defense, without Kawhi Leonard and so spread around the court trying to contain four All-Stars, let McGee roam free and continually find pockets for easy buckets. McGee had 16 points in 10 first half minutes.

"We'll take that from him every night," Durant said.

The Spurs trailed by nine at halftime. But they exited the locker room with some zest. LaMarcus Aldridge, whose dreadful series has frustrated his fanbase and coach, nailed a 3 and spiked through a dunk to cut the Warriors lead to four and force an early third quarter timeout.

Out of the timeout, following a Steph Curry jumper, Durant jumped a passing lane and snagged his second steal, forcefully attacking Danny Green on a fastbreak and powering his way to the free throw line. Durant only made one of the free throws, giving him his first point of the third.

He then slid into the background temporarily, not scoring for the next few minutes as another Spurs run pulled them within 74-71. Some life reentered the building. But it would soon fade.

Starting at the 6:22 mark of the third, Durant took over. He opened his big run with two free throws, then set up a cutting Patrick McCaw — the second round rookie who gave the Warriors great minutes for a second straight game — on a backdoor cut for a floater.

Spurs guard Danny Green tries to defend Kevin Durant, who recorded a game-high 33 points in the Warriors' 120-108 victory. (Jose Carlos Fajardo/Staff)

Durant then attacked Aldridge and forced his way to the line again, his fifth and sixth attempts of the quarter. The free throw parade created a rhythm and soon an eruption.

On the next two possessions, he sharply cut backdoor and finished off two layups set up by David West, who continued his passing renaissance with five assists in 18 minutes. One of those Durant layups included a Jonathon Simmons foul. He made the free throw, giving him seven points in 70 seconds.

"I just thought he got his legs under him and was a little bit more aggressive in his attack," West said.

One possession later, an aggressive Durant continued his onslaught, this time needing no help from teammates. Durant nailed a 24-foot 3 and then, the next time down, planted a 26-footer, plus another foul. He made the free throw, giving him 14 straight Warriors points.

To cap what was a personal 16-7 run, with under three minutes now left in the third quarter, Durant found himself in isolation on Dejounte Murray, the Spurs' backup point guard. He looked around and toward Curry, standing on the opposite side of the court. Curry waved at him to go at Murray, so he did, rising for an impossible to block one-legged fadeaway.

"I just play," Durant said. "If I see a lane open, sometimes I think too much. Sometimes I look to pass when I should look to score. Sometimes I look to score when I should pass. But I figured out if I just don't think at all, that's when I'm best."

The one-legger gave Durant 16 straight Warrior points and 19 of his game-high 33 in the third quarter. By the time he was done, the Warriors were up 18 — 98-80 — and the Spurs were all but vanquished. The Durant takeover was similar to a year before, while with the Thunder, when he completely flipped their second-round series against the Spurs with a monster 17-point fourth quarter in Game 4 to carry his team home.

The Spurs wouldn't win another game in that series. They may not win one at all in this series, thanks, in part, to Durant's massive third quarter in Game 3.

"(We) competed really well," Gregg Popovich said. "Couldn't ask any more from them competitiveness-wise. We turned it over, Kevin Durant had his way for a period there in transition and it just really spread the game open." ■

Spurs big man LaMarcus Aldridge attempts to block Kevin Durant's shot in the third quarter, but the Warriors forward scored 16 straight points in the period. (Jose Carlos Fajardo/Staff)

WESTERN CONFERENCE FINALS • GAME 4

MAY 22, 2017 • SAN ANTONIO, TEXAS
WARRIORS 129, SPURS 115

# SWEEPING BEAUTY

## Warriors Finish Off Spurs, Storm into NBA Finals as First Team to Start 12-0 in Playoffs

### By Anthony Slater

This Warriors' postseason stampede through the Western Conference has been defined by dominance, not drama.

The finale stuck to that script in Game 4. The Warriors jumped up early on the wounded Spurs, squashed every mini rally and then ran away, unthreatened, with a 129-115 win to vanquish another overwhelmed opponent, completing a third straight sweep to become the first team in NBA history to start the postseason 12-0.

"You never come into the playoffs thinking you're going to sweep every series," Draymond Green said. "But if we went 4-3, 4-3, 4-3, we'd still be in the same position. It doesn't mean too much. Means we got a little more rest."

This is the Warriors' third straight Western Conference crown — becoming the only franchise other than the Lakers to do that — and, by far, their easiest path of the three. Ten of the Warriors' 12 wins came by double-digits. They won by an average of 16.3 per game. They haven't lost a game since mid-February when all their stars were healthy and active.

The NBA Finals begin on June 1 in Oracle against Cleveland or, much less likely, Boston. Loads of drama and adversity may be awaiting then. But very little stood in their path to this moment.

"I don't really care who we play," Joe Lacob said, then shot a sly grin. "Ok, maybe a slight preference for Cleveland.

After mashing the Blazers and Jazz the first two rounds, the Warriors faced their first and only real Western Conference scare in Game 1 of Round 3. The Spurs led by 25 at one point in Oracle. But Kawhi Leonard's third quarter ankle sprain changed the game and series. The Warriors zapped themselves awake, came back to win that day and then whacked a scarred Spurs team by 36, 12 and 14 the last three games.

In the finale, the Warriors separated early, just as they had done the previous two series. Steph Curry came out hyper aggressive, slithering through the lane for four layups in the first five minutes. Klay Thompson remained way off — missing his first six shots — but the Warriors often only need two of their elite scorers to be on for domination. And Kevin Durant was.

Durant hit six of his first seven shots, combining with Curry for eight layups in the first 16 minutes. The Warriors eased out to a 31-19 first quarter lead, bumping them up to a plus-57 in Game 4 first quarters this postseason. In the closeout in Portland, they blasted off to a 45-22 first quarter. In the closeout in Salt Lake City,

Danny Green was no match for Kevin Durant, who scored 29 points on 10-of-13 shooting, in the 129-115 win. (Jose Carlos Fajardo/Staff)

they popped the Jazz for a 39-17 first quarter.

In Game 4, that lead sat in double-digits almost the entirety of the night, as the Warriors went 18-of-21 in the paint in the first half.

There were a few moments of life from the Spurs and their crowd, who were celebrating the likely end to Manu Ginobili's brilliant career. In the third quarter, the Spurs cut it to 11 and the crowd rose to life.

But Durant set up Curry for a wing 3, which jacked the lead back to 14. A few possessions later, after they'd sliced it briefly back to 10, Durant attacked in the pick-and-roll and nailed an unguardable pull-back 14-footer.

Which was the story of the series. The Spurs, at such a talent disadvantage, clawed and fought to give themselves even a sliver of hope and then the Warriors' stars, with such scoring ease, put their foot back on the gas pedal and spurted away.

Right after the Durant jumper, Draymond Green hit a 3 to bump the lead to 15, Curry nailed a deep contested wing 3 in front of a frustrated Gregg Popovich and then forced his way to the line for two free throws. The lead, 10 just a couple minutes earlier, was back to 20 and any unrealistic comeback hopes had been dashed, thanks mostly to Durant and Curry.

Curry finished the night with 36 points on 14-of-24 shooting, vaulting himself to a third straight Finals appearance. Durant closed with 29 points on 10-of-13, vaulting himself to his first Finals appearance since 2012.

After a fourth quarter that was more about the Manu send-off than the actual game, history was officially made. The Warriors became the first team to begin the postseason with 12 straight wins. But of course, just like last season, history won't feel as sweet without a title to cap it off. And they know that. The celebration was much more subdued than the previous two times they won it.

"Don't get me wrong, we appreciate this opportunity," Curry said. "Thirty teams suit up every year trying to get to this point. Two teams do. So you have to appreciate it, even if we aren't jumping up and down, screaming at the top of our lungs and all that nonsense."

"It's great and everybody's excited about it," Draymond Green said. "But you just see a difference (this year). It's still kind of a business as usual, we're not finished type of attitude." ∎

After becoming the first NBA team to start an offseason with 12 straight victories, the Warriors pose with the trophy awarded for winning the Western Conference Finals. (Jose Carlos Fajardo/Staff)

Warriors legend Chris Mullin hands the trophy to Draymond Green. Golden State earned
the hardware after reaching a third straight NBA Finals. (Jose Carlos Fajardo/Staff)